ESSENTIAL MAPS

for Family Historians

ESSENTIAL MAPS
for Family Historians

Charles Masters

COUNTRYSIDE BOOKS
NEWBURY BERKSHIRE

First published 2009
© Charles Masters 2009

COUNTRYSIDE BOOKS
3 Catherine Road
Newbury, Berkshire

To view our complete range of books,
please visit us at
www.countrysidebooks.co.uk

ISBN 978 1 84674 098 5

To Oscar Wrigley

Designed by Peter Davies, Nautilus Design
Produced through MRM Associates Ltd., Reading
Printed in Thailand

Contents

Acknowledgements

The book would not have appeared without the active help and support of the following local experts who have willingly shared their expertise and generously contributed material: Anne Buchanan (Librarian, Bath Central Library); Geoff Dawe (Chairman of the Two Villages Archive Trust, Milton Keynes); Betty Halse (Local Historian, Levisham) ; David Keeling (Local Historian, Plymouth/Yelverton); David Hicks (Local Historian, Shere); Jean Manco, (Building Historian); Richard Johnston (Honorary Secretary of the Yateley Society); Penny Stokes (Editor of *Berkshire Family History* magazine and expert on Hamstead Marshall); Colin Wells (Local Historian, Winnersh) and Jill Williams (Local Historian, Thorpe).

The following archivists have also gone out of their way to be helpful: Jennifer Butler (Essex Record Office); Sue Donnelly (the LSE); Susan Ellis (Conwy Borough Council Archives); Rita Freedman (York City Archives); Linda Champ, Suzanne Foster, Sarah Lewin and Janet Smith (Hampshire Record Office); Mark Stevens and Lisa Spurrier (Berkshire Record Office).

The source for each map is given in each case, but I would like to separately thank the following: Patrick Mannix of Moto Enterprises; Dan Brown of 'Bath in Time'; Richard Dean of Cartographics; Graeme Barber (for the Shapter map and information); Barbara Karlsson, Chair of the Shere, Gomshall & Peaslake Local History Society; Teresa Gray of Surrey History Centre.

Thanks, too, are due to Martin Ebdon, Ian Maxted and Ann Noyes who have answered questions and have helped to make this book possible.

Introduction

In tracing our ancestors, their homes and their communities, maps are an indispensable resource. They can be used to identify individuals and to explore the economic and social fabric of their everyday lives. Houses, farms, businesses, factories, towns, streets, villages and parishes, many of which have been obliterated by urban and industrial development, can be located in time and space.

Yates' Map of Glamorgan (1799) and Greenwood's Map of Monmouthshire (1830), for instance, can be used to find place-names which appear in the early censuses but have been lost since through industrial development. The parish of Aberystruth in Monmouthshire, for example, became swamped by urban areas like Ebbw Vale, Abertillery and Nantyglo and is now a totally unfamiliar name even to local residents.

Equally, using on-line resources like Multimap (www.multimap.com), together with Thomas Griffith's survey of the Nanteos Estate in the County of Cardigan (1831), one can be surprised to discover that certain fields and boundaries have not changed in shape for the last 177 years!

Maps, importantly, add to our 'sense of place' and throw light on how previous generations lived and worked. Maps are virtually 'windows' on the past and can take us back to the Elizabethan period, when the pioneers of modern map-making, capitalising on the revolution in printing and new surveying techniques, began to offer patrons and the public more realistic and scientifically accurate representations of the landscape.

However, older maps, in particular, are often seen as problematic to use. Coming in all shapes and sizes, using unfamiliar forms of

Maps, importantly, add to our 'sense of place' and throw light on how previous generations lived and worked.

John Speed's 'Map of Newe: castle', (1610). Copper engraving, later hand-coloured. Notice that the scale is in paces (1 pace = 2 strides).

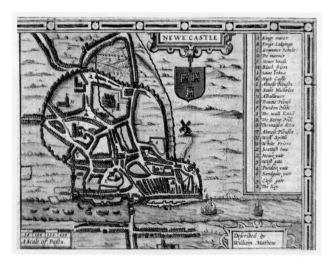

7

measurement and displaying esoteric symbols, maps of an earlier age seem inherently less comprehensible than census or registration records. Yet, used in conjunction with these other records, they add an exciting dimension to the profiling of individuals and communities.

Although there is a technical distinction between what qualifies as a map and what is meant by a plan, I have followed a widespread practice (outside cartographic circles) of making no sharp distinction between the two. Perspective views or 'prospects' of the landscape do not, however, qualify as maps or plans, although maps are themselves often richly pictorial. It was surprisingly common for even the more utilitarian estate maps to sport elaborate cartouches and to contain vignettes of everyday life, or for town maps, like Coussin's plans of Leeds and York, to include, around their margins (or even on the maps themselves), pictorial representations of civic buildings and the houses of the well-to-do in an attempt to please actual, or hoped for, subscribers.

This guide is simply intended to make family historians feel a little more confident when approaching maps as part of their research. The emphasis is on content and the use of English and Welsh maps. The advantages and pitfalls in using particular sorts of maps will be explained but there is no attempt to cover every kind of map or to give a history of cartography – rather the discussion centres on the most useful and accessible types of maps which family historians will want to use.

All About Maps

EVEN A QUICK SURVEY OF THE MAPS AVAILABLE TO FAMILY HISTORIANS REVEALS A BEWILDERING VARIETY WHICH CAN BE DIFFICULT TO INTERPRET AND ASSESS. LATER CHAPTERS ARE DEVOTED TO KEY TYPES OF MAP, BUT IT IS A GOOD IDEA TO BEGIN BY DRAWING ATTENTION TO SOME OF THE MANY KINDS STORED IN PRIVATE, COMMERCIAL AND PUBLIC ARCHIVES. PROPERTY, PLANNING AND EVEN SANITARY RECORDS OF VARIOUS KINDS MAY CONTAIN ACTUAL HOUSE OR FARM PLANS. SALE CATALOGUES, MANY OF WHICH ARE STILL ACTIVELY TRADED ON WEBSITES, NOT INFREQUENTLY CONTAIN PLANS AS WELL AS PROPERTY DESCRIPTIONS AND DETAILS ON SELLERS AND OCCUPIERS.

Wm Dew and Son's 1891 auction catalogue for Ywyddfyd – situated on Great Ormes Head, above Happy Valley at Llandudno – includes both plan and particulars. Said to be in the occupation of William Williams 'as Yearly Tenant', the holding of 21 acres is described in detail. Included in the sale are Y Wyfffyd House with Pasture, outbuildings, a few 'timber-like trees' and part of the mountain! Scribbled in pencil, next to the written particulars, are the actual bids, starting at £400 and rising to £1,250. It appears that the winning bid was made by the tenant himself. The map, at a scale of roughly 25.344 inches to a mile, gives some information on surrounding property, including the nearby quarry and part of the town itself. With the exception of a few prominent landmarks (chapels, hotels and the Pavilion Baths) there is, however, understandably little concern to map or name individual houses along the streets although shading is used to approximately indicate areas of urban settlement.

Large scale maps, especially those produced by the Ordnance Survey (OS), local Boards of Health and the Goad organization (see chapter 5) during the later Victorian period, are likely to allow individual properties to be distinguished and compared with other documentary evidence such as taxation records, censuses and directories. From the time of the Valuation Office Survey of 1910-15 (chapter 7) and, in some cases, from the early days of house numbering, it is possible to positively associate (urban) properties with their house numbers – although, as in the early 20th century, house numbers could alter and the names of streets need not be fixed. In seeking to identify individual properties, maps can often be usefully combined with field work by visiting the area concerned. In some cases, as with Heslington Road in York, the original street name of East Parade is still visible, imprinted on the brickwork of the end house of the terrace.

For the period after the mid 19th century, family historians are most likely to consult the larger scale OS maps which swept aside independent county map-makers and estate map surveyors. Publishers, unable to match the quality and accuracy of these maps, consequently either concentrated on producing reduced scale versions (with the OS turning a blind eye to such efforts) or sought out more specialist markets. Although never totally error free, OS maps were produced to a high standard, using a standardized set of symbols, and can be incredibly detailed. Using, for example, Second World War RAF aerial photographs, together with an 1880s OS map, it is even possible to trace individual trees and avenues of trees, as one historian has recently done for a small area to the east of Reading, in Berkshire. Paradoxically, it is a testament to their influence and importance that OS maps are

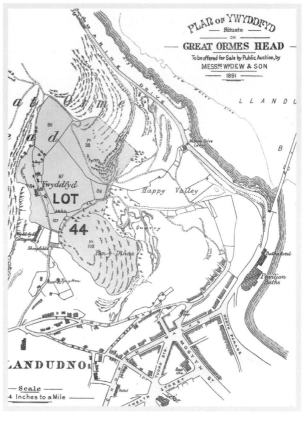

FIGURE I:
Sale Catalogue of Ywyddfyd, Great Orme. Included in the sale was part of Great Orme itself although the vendor reserved the mineral rights under the property for himself. (Conwy Borough Council Archives)

not given separate treatment in this book. Not only is there a definitive guide to these maps already available (*Ordnance Survey maps: a concise guide for historians*, Richard Oliver, 1993), but OS maps are used here to test the reliability of older maps and, in any case, form the basis of both the Valuation Office and National Farm Surveys.

Maps from earlier periods, even when nicely decorated, engraved and (hand) coloured, often seem less inviting to the family historian and undoubtedly have a great many pitfalls for the unwary. On early maps the meanings of descriptive words can vary from map to map. Symbols can be inconsistently used even on the same map, with no supporting key for reference. Scales can be omitted, vary within a map, or use non-standard local measurements. It is not uncommon to find that they failed to follow the familiar convention of having north at the top of the map, and 'north' can be mean due north or even magnetic north! Maps are also often distorted because of the way they were produced, the materials used or simply due to the aging process.

In an age when there was little deterrent in the form of copyright law, maps were shamelessly copied without acknowledgment. Those of the Elizabethan map-maker Saxton and the Stuart map-

Maps from earlier periods, even when nicely decorated, engraved and (hand) coloured, often seem less inviting to the family historian and undoubtedly have a great many pitfalls for the unwary.

DIFFICULT TO DATE

Plagiarism, and the lack of concern to keep copies properly updated, can make maps difficult to date. The year on a map, where given, may not give the true picture of what is shown anyway and topographical features depicted may have to be compared with other sources to try to establish the actual date. Many surveyors and publishers – because of commercial pressures, limits of time and financial worries, or simply out of sheer laziness and expediency – borrowed from earlier maps and knowingly produced second rate publications. Even the surveyors of more official maps, like those for enclosure and tithes, did not always follow high professional standards and freely borrowed from earlier maps. Especially at periods of intense activity, canal and rail maps too could fall short of the required standards, partly for want of experienced surveyors. Many maps found in guidebooks and popular publications, especially during the 19th century, can be next to worthless as reliable and useful sources. Even where the publisher of a directory or guidebook did initially commission a new map, there was no guarantee that it would be updated in later editions.

maker Speed were still being plagiarized and published in the second half of the 18th century, often with little or no revision to reflect changing times. Although their maps, produced on copperplates, were easy to copy, many others were poor and inaccurate facsimiles of the originals.

In family history research no source, of whatever kind, should be taken at face value. One always needs to ask who produced it, for what purpose and when, and maps are no different in this respect.

■ Map-makers

No source should be taken at face value.

Maps were a reflection of not only the skill and experience of a map-maker but his interests as well. **John Rocque**, who died in 1762, was particularly interested in parks and gardens, for example; whilst **John Speed** (1552-1629), like many others, was keen to record antiquities. Although many maps were one-offs produced by unknown map-makers, others, like those of Rocque and Jefferys in the 18th century, were the work of men with a reputation for competence that they were keen to maintain, even at the cost of their own personal financial solvency. This did not mean that their maps did not vary in quality, for all sorts of reasons, but positive scholarly (and contemporary) assessment of such surveyors' skill and commitment is helpful when approaching their work. There were many surveyors not so well known – like **John Blagrave** and **Josiah Ballard** – and without national reputations to defend who nevertheless produced maps of quality for their clients. It, therefore, often pays to find out what one can about the map-maker whose map is being consulted. Sometimes, as in the case of **Richard Horwood**, who produced an outstanding map of London at the end of the 18th century, there is little apart

HUMAN SETTLEMENT

Buildings, settlements and many other features of a landscape may be incidental to a map-maker concerned with producing a map of landholding. Houses may be over- or under-represented and settlements merely conventionally and stylistically drawn. Many estate maps fall into this category – though not all. The maps drawn of mid 18th-century Tavistock, for instance, by the agent of the Duke of Bedford, show that landowners often had an interest in the accurate mapping of settlement as well. Nevertheless, the general point stands that estate and similar maps concerned with land ownership will tend to under-record human settlement and other forms of human activity (including industrial), unless the landowner sponsoring the map has a particular stake in such activity.

A MAP'S PURPOSE

An understanding of the purpose of a map or plan is essential if its strengths and weaknesses are to be assessed.

The purposes for which a map is produced can be very diverse. Spry's Plot of 1584 is concerned to show the projected course of the Plymouth Leat from its head weir on the River Meavy (Mewy) down to Plymouth. The hinterland is, at best, a cross between illustration and diagram. Names of villages, a few major connecting tracks and the principal rivers are shown, but not accurately, although the overall relationships are more or less correct. Tudor defence plans can equally show local settlement almost as an afterthought, but may still represent the only 'visual' record available. Transport plans, deposited with Parliament by turnpike, canal and railway companies during the 18th and 19th centuries, are not concerned with recording the landscape as such, but nevertheless can reliably include information on the owners of properties along any proposed route, many of whom were selling land to the companies or were affected by 'demolition' orders (see figs.2 and 3).

from the map itself to judge him by. Not only is little known about this map-maker, but he produced only one other map (a study of Liverpool) before he died somewhat prematurely in 1803.

County map-makers, operating on a much smaller scale, were obviously constrained in what they could show, although for sound financial reasons they often marked the seats and houses of the gentry – if necessary, at the expense of other information. Town map-makers, similarly, could be more concerned to flatter the vanity of civic leaders and potential sponsors and to show the general layout of a town, with its network of streets, than to plot houses and their layouts in detail, Less attractive features of the landscape, like a cholera burial ground or area of slum housing, could even disappear from a survey through deliberate, rather than accidental, omission.

No attempt can be made here to chart the history of cartography but it is important to realize that modern scientific map-making dates only from Tudor times and the discovery and gradual application of new surveying techniques. Medieval and earlier maps are few and far between and are invariably symbolic, moral and aesthetic creations, with little or no relationship to reality on the ground. It is no coincidence that the earliest maps and plans that are discussed in this book date from the late 16th century onwards. The maps of such pioneers as Saxton and Speed still inform our understanding of past landscapes, despite their many defects. Saxton, whose ground-breaking county maps have resulted in him being described as the father of English cartography, went on to produce estate maps

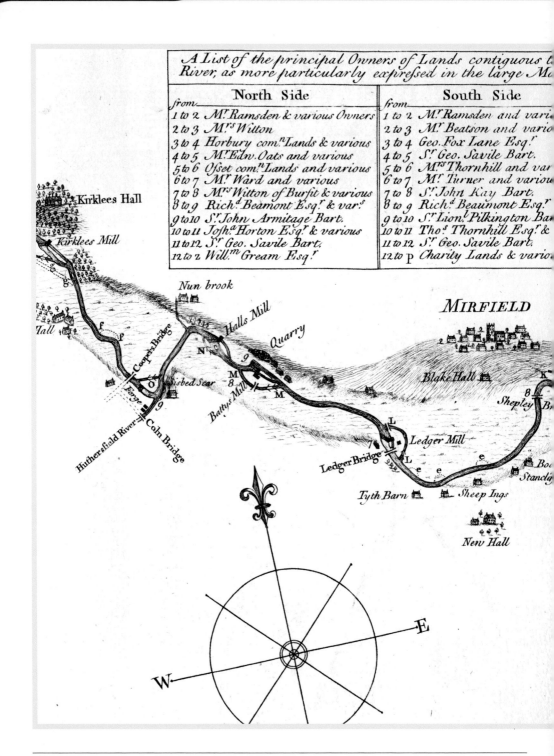

A List of the principal Owners of Lands contiguous t[o] River, as more particularly expressed in the large Ma[p]

North Side		South Side	
from		from	
1 to 2	Mr. Ramsden & various Owners	1 to 2	Mr. Ramsden and vari[ous]
2 to 3	Mrs. Witton	2 to 3	Mr. Beatson and vario[us]
3 to 4	Horbury comnt. Lands & various	3 to 4	Geo. Fox Lane Esqr.
4 to 5	Mr. Edw. Oats and various	4 to 5	Sr. Geo. Savile Bart.
5 to 6	Ofset comnt. Lands and various	5 to 6	Mrs. Thornhill and var[ious]
6 to 7	Mr. Ward and various	6 to 7	Mr. Turner and variou[s]
7 to 8	Mrs. Witton of Burfit & various	7 to 8	Sr. John Kay Bart.
8 to 9	Richd. Beamont Esqr. & vars.	8 to 9	Richd. Beaumont Esqr.
9 to 10	Sr. John Armitage Bart.	9 to 10	Sr. Lionl. Pilkington Ba[rt.]
10 to 11	Josha. Horton Esqr. & various	10 to 11	Thos. Thornhill Esqr. & [various]
11 to 12	Sr. Geo. Savile Bart.	11 to 12	Sr. Geo. Savile Bart.
12 to 2	Willm. Gream Esqr.	12 to p	Charity Lands & vario[us]

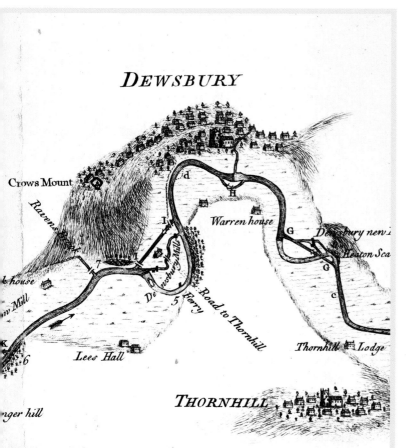

DEWSBURY

Crows Mount

Ravens

house

w Mill

K

6

nger hill

Warren house

Lees Hall

THORNHILL

Dewsbury new

Heaton Sca

Road to Thornhill

Thornhill Lodge

		The following Shoals or Streams are to be dredged, and some of them weared or walled where necessary. —
a	C	From the Brook to the Tail of Horbury Cutt.
b	F	A Stream below the Figure of 3-Lock Cutt.
c		A Stream below Dewsbury new Mill.
d		Water-gate Stream.
e e e		3 covered Shoals between Mirfield low Mill and Ledger M
f f		Lyon Royd Stream.
g g		From below the Island to the Tail of Kirklees Cutt.
+		A covered Shoal in Kirklees-mill Dam.
h h		Willow and Lee Streams.
i		A covered Shoal between Brighouse and Brooksfoot Wood
k		Cromwell bottom Streams.
l		Upper part of Long Stream.
m Y		From the Tail of Raland-mill Grait to the Tail of the Cutt

FIGURE 2:
'A Plan of the River Calder from Wakefield to...Hebble Bridge' by John Smeaton, 1757. Prepared to show the intended arrangements for making the river navigable, it schedules the landowners affected on each side. This waterway, the Calder & Hebble Navigation, was opened in 1765. Map engraved by R. W. Seale, 33 x 11 inches, scale two inches to the mile. (Canalmaps Archive; www.canalmaps.net)

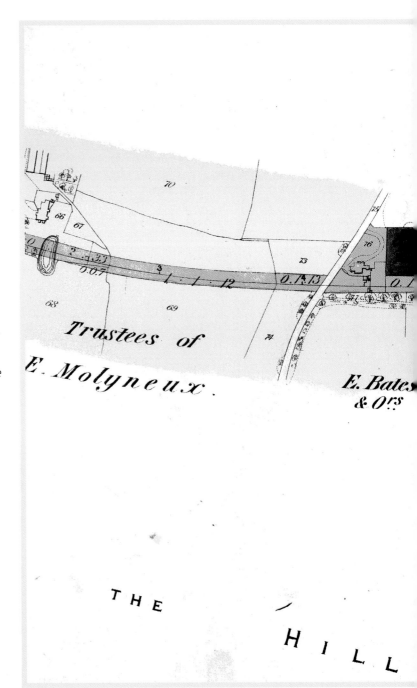

FIGURE 3:
1874 Survey of the proposed Liverpool North Extension of the Cheshire Lines Railway through the village of West Derby. Names of affected landowners (recorded in a separate schedule) have been endorsed by hand on this copy and their holdings coloured. The railway opened in 1879. Lithographed, scale six chains to the inch. (Cartographics Archive; www. cartographics.co.uk)

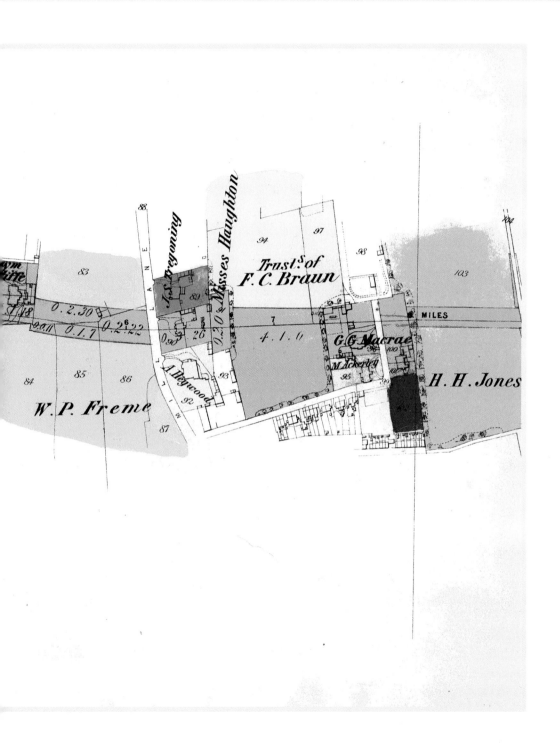

which are still worth consulting. John Speed, who collected together some of the best work of Elizabethan map-makers in his bestselling 'Theatre' county atlas of 1611-12, included, as inserts on these county maps, what were often the first town maps of the places depicted. The majority were the work of Speed himself who, like Saxton before him, saw the value in direct observation of the landscape. And if figures like Saxton and Speed are still seen as the giants of English cartography, there are many 18th- and 19th-century map-makers of note, of whom Rocque, Jefferys, Horwood and, for the early 19th century, Christopher Greenwood, are amongst some of the better known.

In approaching the maps of both famous and lesser known map-makers, certain rules of thumb and a dose of commonsense go a long way. Larger scale maps are likely to be more detailed than ones on a smaller scale, although some of the best large-scale maps favoured a minimalist approach and a focus on the task at hand. Homespun creations, especially of an early date, may be exactly that, but can nevertheless be as accurate as later finely decorated or engraved ones – which are apt to say as much about the publisher as the map-maker. Maps by prolific and professional mapmakers are not necessarily more accurate than those of amateurs who produced one or two maps as a sideline from their main job.

In terms of locating maps, the Internet is obviously a good starting point. It offers not only on-line and interactive access to modern maps but also, increasingly, collections of historical maps of all kinds.

Although much can be learned about the purpose and quality of a map by analysing its content, maps should always be compared with other sources (including other maps) whenever possible. Issues of scale and likely accuracy can often be addressed by comparison with later OS maps of the same area. In many cases, much can be learned by field work and the use of photographs. Many present-day roads, streets, boundaries and houses can be traced back to earlier maps – at least outside large urban and industrial areas.

■ Locating maps

In terms of locating maps, the Internet is obviously a good starting point. It offers not only on-line and interactive access to modern maps but also, increasingly, collections of historical maps of all kinds.

Many maps can be found locally, through visiting the local reference library or contacting a local record office or historical society.

The Northumberland Communities Project (run by the Northumberland Archives Service) and the 'enclosures' website of the Berkshire Record Office show what record offices, libraries, museums and similar bodies can achieve in this respect. The websites of local historical societies, like Milton Keynes' Two Villages Trust, illustrate how maps can be used to explore a community's past. A number of commercial websites are run by companies who have an in-depth knowledge of the maps on offer and provide a good choice of images online.

Many maps can be found locally, through visiting the local reference library or contacting a local record office or historical society. It is always wise to contact a holding well in advance of visiting to ensure a particular map is available, although York Reference Library, for example, has a long series of maps which can be easily consulted on arrival and without prior appointment. Increasingly, even where originals can only be found in national collections, there will be photocopies or digital copies held locally.

Inevitably, access to maps is not always easy. They may be in the hands of private landowners and institutions, or to be found only in national or specialist collections. The Valuation Office and National Farm Surveys (chapters 7 and 8), for instance, are housed in The National Archives at Kew and, unlike enclosure

Inevitably, access to maps is not always easy.

and tithe maps, it is unlikely that a local society will have examples of material of this kind to consult, either in person or online.

As can be seen in the sources/further reading at the end of the respective chapters, there are now good finding aids, especially for enclosure and tithe maps. Many maps, however, are still not adequately catalogued, even in public collections, or remain to be discovered. In the case of Ditton Priors in Shropshire, an important estate map – dating from 1768 – was only recently found in the attic of an old farmhouse once belonging to a land agent working for the estate concerned. It is now proudly displayed in the local health centre!

———————●●———————

County Maps

COUNTY MAPS, MORE THAN ANY OTHER GENRE, LAUNCHED THE MODERN AGE IN MAP-MAKING AND REMAINED A MAINSTAY OF MAP PUBLISHING UNTIL SUPERSEDED BY THE LARGE-SCALE OS MAPS OF THE 19TH CENTURY. THE SMALL SCALE OF COUNTY MAPS, INEVITABLY MEANS THAT IMPORTANT DETAIL IS OMITTED AND THERE IS MUCH SCOPE FOR GENERALIZATION. SETTLEMENTS ARE OFTEN POORLY REPRESENTED AND INDIVIDUAL PROPERTIES (APART FROM CERTAIN 'SEATS' OF THE GENTRY AND BUILDINGS LIKE CHURCHES) CAN BE IMPOSSIBLE TO TRACE.

Benjamin Donn, in his Devon map of 1765, was more concerned than most of his contemporaries to map settlements but Yelverton ('Elvertown') is shown as a single building when it was, by this time, a collection of small dwellings around the original large house. He was also willing to give space to miniature drawings of the homes of the gentry (shown in elevation) at the expense of other detail. With rare exceptions, like Martyn's map of Cornwall (1748), parish boundaries are not mapped until the Greenwood maps of the early 19th century. Greenwood, however, still arbitrarily straightened out these boundaries, making them less authoritative. Place-names were often not recorded, or were based on the (misheard) testimony of locals.

Yet even the primitive efforts of the Elizabethan map-makers, like Saxton and Speed, are too readily dismissed as being of little value. Christopher Saxton, the best known if not perhaps the most skilled of the band of Elizabethan pioneers that also included Norden and Smith, started producing his series of county maps for England and Wales in 1574 and published his landmark atlas of 34 maps in 1579. Although he drew on cartographic and other sources, his maps were also based on direct observation and involved sketching the actual landscape from vantage points such as church towers. Whilst not even major road routes are marked – an omission addressed by some later copyists and publishers – many topographical features (physical and man-made) such as settlements, rivers, hills, woods, bridges, lakes and parks are recorded with some degree of accuracy. An approximate idea of the relative size of settlements can be gleaned from the size of lettering used for place-names and the fact that large towns have collections of houses and churches, whilst many of the smaller places are shown merely by means of a circle with a dot inside. 'Molehills' were drawn to indicate relief, and hand-colouring was done to help distinguish the various topographical features.

Family historians are better served by the host of more 'scientifically' surveyed maps that appeared during the 18th and early 19th centuries, in what proved to be the heyday of county map-making.

Despite the merits of such maps, there is no question that family historians are better served by the host of more 'scientifically' surveyed maps that appeared during the 18th and early 19th centuries, in what proved to be the heyday of county map-making. Between 1700 and 1840, 120 county maps at the very useful scale of one inch to the mile or greater were produced, with every county in England eventually having at least one such large-scale map. Although later 18th-century efforts – often produced with a Society of Arts prize in mind – tend to be more accurate and detailed than earlier ones, there are many notable exceptions, such as Henry Beighton's very creditable early 18th-century map of Warwickshire. Map-makers of note include John Rocque and Thomas Jefferys for the 18th century and the Greenwood brothers for the early 19th century. Jefferys was a London-based publisher who had previously worked on revisions of Saxton's maps! For his Yorkshire county map, published in 1771–2, he was careful to employ local surveyors, and, although earlier maps and plans were consulted, the land was surveyed using a range of up-to-date and well-tested techniques. Comparison with a later OS map of the same area shows a good standard of accuracy.

Example: **Rocque's county maps of Berkshire and Surrey**

John Rocque's work reveals, quite clearly, what some of the better quality county maps can offer to the family historian. A Huguenot émigré, who came to work in Britain in the 1730s as a kind of upmarket garden and park designer, his portfolio of work included maps of both Berkshire and Surrey.

As his Berkshire map shows, he generally specialized in maps produced on individual sheets rather than in atlases (although a small atlas published in the 1750s did quite well). His *Topographical Survey of the County of Berkshire*, finally published in 1761 but commenced a decade earlier, comprises 18 sheets and, remarkably, there is a helpful, separately published, key sheet. The comparatively large scale of two inches to a mile allowed him to show not only the seats of the gentry and nobility and well-known landmarks, but also the landscape and human settlement in great detail. This included the depiction of settlements of all sizes (down to hamlets and individual farms and cottages); natural features like rivers, hills, valleys and woods; various communication routes (man-made or otherwise); and a limited selection of 'industrial' sites (notably mills). His interest in land use was unusual and led him to show arable and grassland, commons and downland, with an attempt to include both the extent of fields (open and enclosed) and parish boundaries. The attention to detail was such that he recorded mile markers (indicating a coaching route) and, of more interest to family historians, individual houses (marked as small rectangles) and hedges. This means, for example, that a family historian using this source might be able to locate not only the settlement in which an ancestor lived, but perhaps even (with the help of other documentary or field evidence) the location of his or her house!

Map-makers and their surveyors could be quite idiosyncratic and inconsistent in what they chose to record.

Yet whatever the Rocque map purports to show, how trustworthy is this map of Berkshire in practice? As we have seen, map-makers and their surveyors could be quite idiosyncratic and inconsistent in what they chose to record. It would be unreasonable, of course, to demand the level of accuracy of a modern Ordnance Survey map and mistakes arising from the surveying or printing process could, and, inevitably, did occur. Nevertheless, the question of its accuracy remains.

On the positive side, some reassurance is offered by the fact that Rocque employed the local surveyor Josiah Ballard, who went on to make several well regarded estate maps of the Reading area, including the 1756 map of the manor of Earley.

IN-DEPTH STUDIES

In-depth studies of the Hamstead Marshall and Winnersh areas of Berkshire shown on the Rocque maps (figs.5 and 6) have raised the strong possibility that some houses, at least, were schematically drawn rather than true depictions. For the family historian, anxious to trace a particular house, as well as a settlement, the accuracy of such maps in this respect is of more than academic interest!

For instance, within the Chapel Corner area of Hamstead Marshall lies the former Craven estate house called 'The Holding' (fig.7). The house has the design, proportions and – most importantly – the roof structure of a classic Georgian two-up, two-down, suggesting strongly that the property may have been standing at the time of Rocque's survey. Although there is a strong suspicion from what is known of the area that Rocque depicts too many houses in the cluster around the Chapel Corner site, an estate survey map and schedule from 1775 seem to confirm that a house, if not this house, was sited as shown by Rocque. For the record, the house can also be traced in the enclosure award map of 1815, and again in the tithe map of 1840, as the house, workshop and saw yard passed down through generations of the Burton family whose menfolk served as carpenters and wheelwrights to the Craven estate.

And, as with other maps and map-makers, Rocque would have invited the local gentry and other interested parties to point out errors at the proof stage. On the negative side, the map was a commercial production with all the pressures that this brought.

Although Thomas Pride's later, 1790 map of the Reading area (fig.4) shows a remarkable degree of similarity with Rocque's work in terms of houses, roads, rivers and woods, it is quite possible that Pride's work is derivative of Rocque's and subject to the same errors! Modern research has convincingly shown that Rocque's field boundaries – and not only in his Berkshire map – were apt to be too large or even fictitious, although he seems to have been more willing than Thomas Pride to sub-divide fields!

Research in the Thorpe area of Surrey, using Rocque's Surrey map (fig.8), suggests that this map is likely to be of service to the family historian. The most populated areas may be the most accurately surveyed but the plot positions of cottages seem reasonably accurate. Overlaying the Rocque map on a modern OS map shows that the majority of roads are correctly located,

FIGURE 4: *Pride's Map of Reading and adjoining country 'to the Extent of Ten Miles'. The map, which is dedicated to Lord Craven and has its left and right borders decorated with various coats of arms, includes the seats of the nobility and gentry like Basildon Park and Englefield Park.* (Berkshire Record Office)

FIGURE 5: *Rocque's Map of Berkshire 1761, section showing Hamstead Marshall.* (Berkshire Record Office)

FIGURE 6: *Rocque's Map of Berkshire 1761, section showing King Street area, Winnersh.* (Berkshire Record Office)

except in the Thorpe Lea area where they are distorted. Since it is known that land was taken out of common field use to create sites for large mansion houses, this may partly (though not fully) account for any discrepancy. The OS map also shows that Rocque's scale is slightly out. A distance of 7.091 miles from Windsor Castle's round tower to Thorpe church on the OS map measures only 6.202 miles on Rocque's map. The course of the River Thames is also not drawn accurately in all respects. Place-names are mostly correct – allowing for local variations in spelling – although Runneymede is called Lunny Mead!

FIGURE 7: 'The Holding' at Hamstead Marshall. (Courtesy Penny Stokes)

As far as parish boundaries are concerned, an inspection of the Winnersh area shows a close match between Rocque's Berkshire map and the outline as given on the 1844 enclosures map. However, there are two important differences. In the first place, the Rocque map shows the top boundary going along what is now Sandford Lane, whereas the enclosures boundary goes further north to include the large mansion at Whistley. The second difference is at the bottom of the parish, where Rocque's line goes further to the south-west than the enclosures map to include Newland. The lack of other contemporary sources makes it impossible to determine whether these were errors or just changes in the boundaries in the intervening period. As boundary changes they make a good deal of sense.

Rocque's work, whilst clearly not perfect, compares well with that of many of his contemporaries who lacked his measure of skill, or scruples, or simply succumbed to commercial pressures.

The later 18th-century 'Map of Surrey' by Joseph Lindley and William Crosley is, in fact, a copy of Rocque's earlier map, whilst Stephen Pyle's Leicestershire map of 1777 is a copy of Morden's much earlier one of 1695. Horsley and Coy's map of Northumberland was so riddled with mistakes that it became necessary to publish a set of corrections. Even more careful efforts like that of John Prior, with his county map of Leicestershire (1779), offer a less than reliable survey of individual villages and farms.

Such maps were, unfortunately, often drawn on by subsequent map-makers and publishers. John Cary, for instance, who produced his first county atlas in 1787 and whose maps were printed over and over again, drew on the work of Prior! Eventually, of course, in the 19th century, the OS was to overwhelm the efforts of even the best independent county map-makers. The early 19th-century, large-scale, county maps by the prolific Christopher Greenwood – often of good quality – already looked similar to the OS variety. Thomas Moule, perhaps recognizing where he might still find a market, went for highly decorative maps instead.

■ Locating the maps

Perhaps surprisingly, images of many of the county maps, even those by Saxton and Speed, are to be found on a number of websites for viewing and even purchase. Copies of the 19th-century maps by such map-makers as Greenwood and Moule are also relatively easy to obtain. The publisher Harry Margary has produced facsimiles of some of the better known, or frequently used, county maps and these can often be found in university libraries. County record offices and libraries are likely to have one or more original copies of their main county maps.

The Northumberland Communities website includes county maps of Northumberland and is an excellent resource (http://communities.northumberland.gov.uk/).

Mostlymaps of Hay-on-Wye is both a shop and website and is one of my favourite commercial sources for Saxton and Speed maps (www.mostlymaps.com).

FIGURE 8: *Rocque's Map of Surrey. Only the Thorpe and Thorpe Green areas are shown.* (Surrey History Centre)

Estate Surveys

Our pre-Victorian ancestors were more likely to be living and working in small rural communities than in London or the provincial towns. The search for our rural ancestors is greatly assisted by the survival of relatively large numbers of estate maps in public or private collections, which may cover a location of interest.

Characteristically drawn on a large scale, estate maps can be of an individual farm, part of a parish, a whole parish, several parishes, or detached areas across one or more counties. For very large estates, the maps constituting a single complete survey can be found collected together in one or more volumes of maps and accompanied by books of reference. Although often decorated with elaborate cartouches and even pictorial scenes, estate maps often appear more utilitarian than published maps which had to appeal to both subscribers and the public and were often expertly engraved. From the parish or village perspective, the quality of a map has more to do with the wealth or fastidiousness of the sponsor than the size or population of the parish, or the extent and significance of estate holdings contained within it.

Estate surveys are a key source for our understanding of rural life.

Whether crudely or finely drawn, elaborately decorated or not, in good condition or otherwise, estate surveys are a key source for our understanding of rural life. Estate surveys were often used without acknowledgement by the makers of both enclosure and tithe maps. They can vary enormously in the detail they record, but are invariably large scale and may be accompanied by one or more tables of reference – either on the map itself or produced separately.

One can expect fields and their boundaries to be recorded,

with field names and acreages. Greater or lesser detail will be given of hedges, walls, fences and ditches and other boundary markers such as streams, rivers, roads and paths. In many cases, the names of tenants and lessees of the land are given (often in a table), together with the names of adjacent landowners. Prominent buildings like the manor and farm houses may be depicted (perhaps in elevation). Open fields, where they survived, may be included, together with the owners' names. Other features of the human and physical landscape, such as commons, meadow, heath, orchards, gardens, trees, copses, woodland, mills and other sites of industry, will be recorded if the surveyor and the estate owner considered them important. The tables or books of reference gave the opportunity to record

BEWARE THE ACCURACY OF ESTATE MAPS

Early examples of estate maps, dating from the late 16th and 17th centuries, frequently draw the principal properties in perspective view and can be deceptively amateurish in style. A survey and description of Southcott manor in Berkshire, belonging to Anthony Blagrave, is a pertinent example (fig. 9). No scale is given, in fact, but the map was drawn at approximately 13 inches to the mile. Remarkably, it was drawn by Anthony's brother, John Blagrave, who describes himself as a 'gent'.

Surrounded by an indenture giving additional handwritten information on the Blagraves, the coloured map is quite detailed. The manor farm and farm buildings are shown in elevation and the map includes fields (with their names and acreage), paddock, meadow, routes (including lanes and 'London Hygh Waye'), watercourses, bridges (with a clapper bridge shown crossing the River Kennet) and 'Coomber Ditche'. The map even shows part of the 'higher feylde', which had recently been sold, and gives the name of the purchaser. The impression the casual observer of the map might gain is that, although the surveyor might be very familiar with the estate because of his personal connection, the map may not be even tolerably accurate. Yet a 6-inch OS map of the area, drawn some 300 years later, seems to show that field boundaries had changed little in the interval!

Although, in general, later 18th-century or early 19th-century maps are often more accurately drawn, this is far from being universally the case. It is also important to remember that differences in field boundaries between an estate or parish map and a later OS map do not necessarily mean that the earlier survey is incorrect. It is often worthwhile to try to compare an earlier map with one drawn a little later, although it is possible that the surveyor of the later map knew of, and had access to, the earlier map himself!

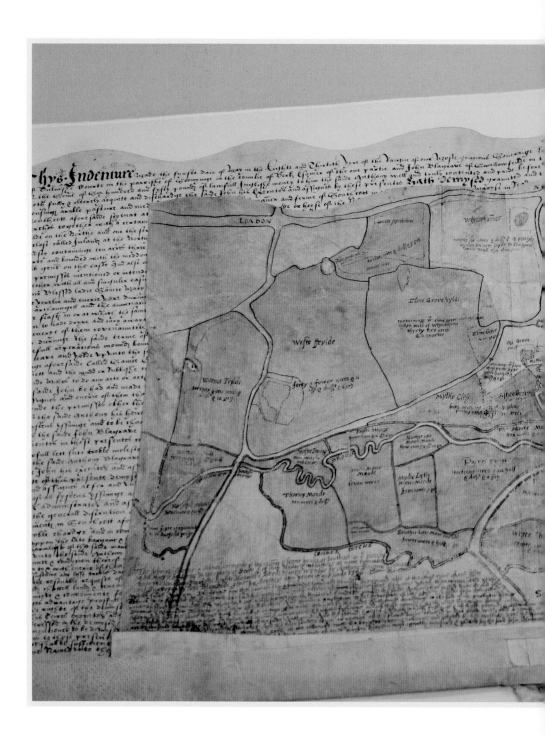

FIGURE 9: *Survey of the Manor of Southcott, Reading, 1596 by John Blagrave. Map with separate explanatory indenture. (Berkshire Record Office)*

more details about the holdings and landscape and are often crucial in interpreting the map itself. They were sometimes stored separately from the map and, consequently, may be missing.

Since the focus is on land ownership, settlements and less important buildings in the area could be ignored altogether, or conventionally drawn with little concern for accurate depiction or siting. Yet this is not the whole story. Estates often covered urban as well as rural areas. Just as a landowner with a lead mine on his land might wish to have it mapped thoroughly, the same can be true regarding a landowner and a town or village. Tavistock is an excellent example of a town carefully mapped in the 18th century for the local landowner – in this case the Duke of Bedford. Here colour is carefully used to distinguish the various owners of buildings and gardens. A very small percentage of estate surveys, too, are what are called 'house and estate surveys'. Examples include the 17th-century estate surveys of the Devon landowner John Willoughby. These can give great detail on every house, even listing and naming the rooms and giving house sizes.

Estates often covered urban as well as rural areas.

An early estate map of the Manor of Milton in Surrey, dating from 1659, can be assessed using Rocque's later county map and local knowledge. For the purposes of comparison, the focus is on the parishes of Egham and Thorpe in Surrey – it is one of the strengths of manor surveys that they do not necessarily end at parish boundaries. The coloured map itself was produced for Corpus Christi, Oxford, who still have the map in their archives. Its rather crude style is in keeping with its early date. The scale is rather peculiar and, like many older maps, North is not at the top. It shows property, fields, roads and land use (such as pasture, arable and wood). The road layout, as well as field sizes and location, seems to be very similar to Rocque's map. Indeed, overlaying one on top of the other gives quite a good fit. From what is known of soil types and farm layouts in the area, the map seems fairly accurate. Several drawings in elevation are given. Although simply drawn, one of the houses standing today appears similar to its drawing. Unfortunately, the manor house, which is the subject of quite a detailed drawing, was later demolished. Where, on the map, concentrations of property exist, orientation is good; however, isolated cottages are impossible to locate because there is insufficient detail.

Compared to the Blagrave and Manor of Milton surveys, the 1756 map of the Whiteknights estate owned by Sir Henry Englefield (shown here in its fine reduced copy form of 1826 – fig.10) seems a far more professional survey. Its surveyor was none other than Josiah Ballard, the local estate surveyor employed by Rocque when working on his county map of Berkshire. A red line is used to delineate the extent of the survey. The map, which includes coverage of the whole of the Liberty of Earley in Sonning Parish, also shows boundaries formed by the River Thames on one side and the River Lodden on the other, as well as plot boundaries, roads, paths, rivers, heathland, meadow and wood. To the north there is evidence of 'old' enclosure (which, as in so many cases, was actually a recent event). Letters are used to link the plots or 'closes' of tenants to a reference table and detail is given of acreages and to whom tenants paid their tithes. The four listed tithe owners include the 'Deanery of Sunning'. Neighbouring landowners shown include a Mrs Price.

A FINE EXAMPLE

Whilst Ballard's Whiteknights map is well-crafted, there are numbers of estate surveys which are both rich in detail and cover large areas. A fine example of this is Bernard Scale's 1778 estate survey of the lands of Richard Rigby. The estate, covering parts of Essex and Suffolk and consisting of well over 6,000 acres, includes Mistley manor and the 'town' of Mistley Thorn. The survey of the estate is made up of 31 maps, each with its own separate table of reference. Details recorded include the names of tenants, field names, land use and the names of adjoining property. Colour is also used on the maps to indicate the state of cultivation.

The map of Mistley Thorn (fig.11), at a scale of 40 inches to the mile, shows a community in close-up. Villagers' plots are drawn in such a way that it is clear that some observation has taken place and they are linked by plot number to a separate table of reference (fig.12) which lists the name of each tenant and the size and character of each holding. Dwellings are distinguished from other kinds of premises by colouring them red. Local landmarks shown include the church and the green. The importance to the town of its riverside location (by the River Stour) is shown by the attention given to the quay and its facilities and the careful depiction of the ships at, or near, the quayside.

FIGURE 10: *Plan of Earley Whiteknights – the estate of Sir Henry Englefield (1756); reduced copy, 1826, by J. and W. Newton. One of the neighbouring landowners given is a Mr Blagrave!* (Berkshire Record Office)

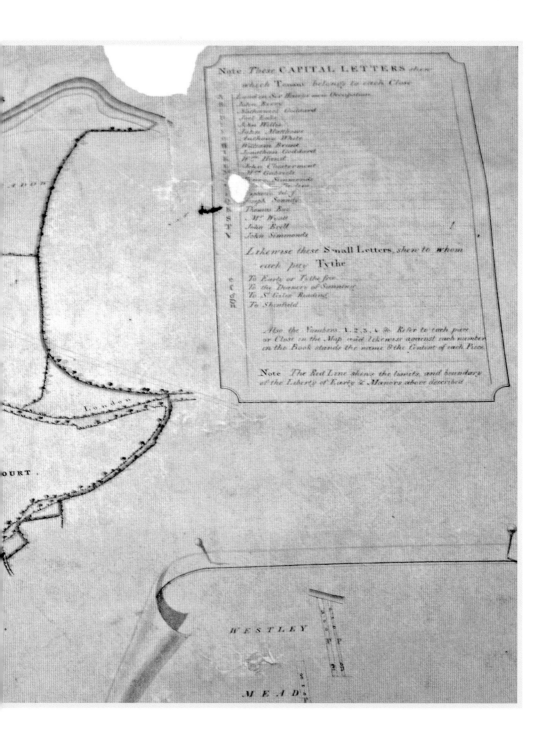

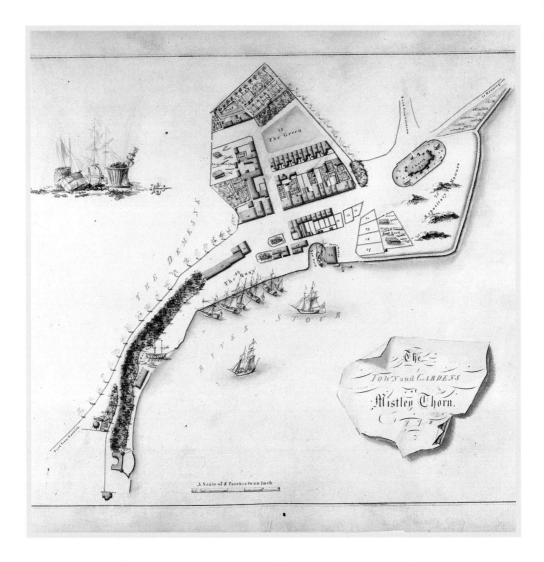

FIGURE II: *Survey of Mistley Thorn map by Bernard Scale, 1778. Notice the prominence given to the riverside and shipping.* (Essex Record Office)

FIGURE 12: *Survey of Mistley Thorn reference table by Bernard Scale, 1778.* (Essex Record Office)

There are, of course, many parishes and manors for which there is no pre-19th-century estate map. Either none was made in the first place, or it may be that a particular survey has been lost or destroyed. In any case, manors are not the same as parishes and a survey can give an incomplete or misleading view of landownership and occupation at the parish level.

Most estate maps remained in manuscript, although more than one copy was generally made. Sometimes, where land has remained in the same hands for generations, a sequence of such maps can be found. For the parish of Ditton Priors, for instance, where parliamentary enclosure did not occur until the 19th century, the 1768 estate map, with accompanying rental survey, presents an invaluable snapshot of tenants and their farms at this date.

SHERE, SURREY

The village of Shere in Surrey has no enclosure map either for the 18th or 19th centuries. This is not altogether surprising as places that have a tithe award – such as Shere – quite often do not have an enclosure map. The reverse case is even more likely since enclosure often extinguished tithes (see chapter 6). Even so, family historians are advised not to assume that this is the case in their particular locality. Fortunately, Shere village is blessed with a number of estate maps covering the later 18th and early 19th centuries, as well as a parish map of 1823 (based, it appears, on a Greenwood map). William Bray's large 1772 map of Shere (fig.13) – which shows two dwellings (including High House Farm) in elevation and the estate lands – was drawn up at a time when William Bray was extending his holdings by acquiring (through purchase) small areas of land like South ('Soutt') Field which had formerly been common land. The map shows the fields with their names and, by means of a table of reference, their acreages and use. The much smaller Hooker estate map of 1798, which shows some areas in the village, acts as a useful complement to the earlier Bray map and aligns well with the OS 6-inch map.

Milton Keynes village is one that is reliant on estate and parish maps. Unlike the neighbouring village of Broughton, it was not on a turnpike, nor was it close enough to a canal or railway to feature on transport maps. The 1789 map (fig.14) was reconstructed from an original estate map of 1782 made for George Finch, Fourth Earl of Nottingham and Ninth Earl of Winchelsea. The date of 1789 has been chosen to tie in with

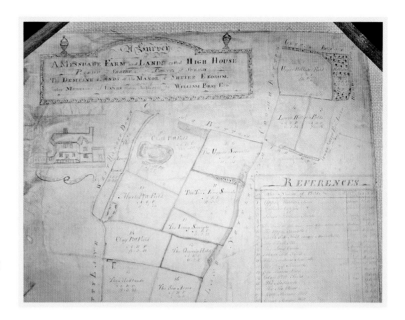

For the many areas where enclosure records are absent or lost (or of a late date), locating an estate map can be of added significance.

FIGURE 13: *William Bray's 1772 map of the Bray Estate.* (Courtesy Shere Museum)

FIGURE 14: *Milton Keynes 'Parishfields' map, 1789.* (Courtesy Two Villages Trust)

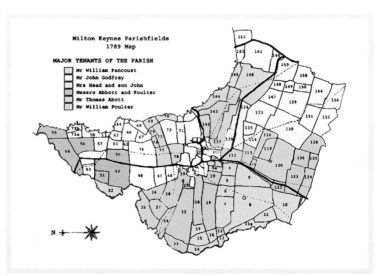

a sale catalogue of that date which lists the tenants. The original map, which was not coloured, gives field names together with plot numbers for each field. Tenants' names are not given but field names like 'Abbott's March Meadow' and 'Poulter's March Meadow' are suggestive. In the 1789 survey these are both shown as 'March Meadow', but Abbott has been replaced by Godfrey. As always with early maps, care must be taken to check the orientation! Several of the field names, like Wrens Park, Great Linch and Kingsoe Lays, have been used for the names of recent roads although, often, these roads are not that close to the locations they are named after.

FIGURE 15: *Bird's Cottage.* (Courtesy Two Villages Trust)

Information on Milton Keynes families named in the sale catalogue can be drawn from the church registers of baptisms, marriages and burials which run from 1559. Among the families listed in 1789 were the Birds and Abbotts. The Abbotts, who appear in parish records from 1684 to 1838, were a farming family holding a comparatively small amount of land. There is a cottage in the village still called Abbot's Cottage but which once was known by the more meaningful name of Abbot's Close.

The Bird family appears in the parish records from 1684 to 1985. They were mostly engaged in building work for the estate owners, the Finch family, and their tenant farmers. A cottage known as Bird's Cottage (fig.15), of which there is fortunately a late 19th-century photograph, is situated next to the old school building in the village. It is thought to be one of the oldest buildings in North Buckinghamshire, and to be one of the two manor houses in the village. Its timber-frame construction is that of a 'cruck', and a number of years ago, when it was re-thatched, it was found that the old thatch had smoke blackening on the inside. This, together with the evidence of the timber frame, indicates that at one time it was a hall house with an open fire and simply a hole in the roof to let out the smoke. It was much modified by the Birds in their capacity as builders and does not look from the outside to be particularly old.

Another long-resident family – the Heads – must have been reasonably well off since one of the family graves was a large tomb chest with railings. Although there are other cases of families remaining in the village, or close by, for generations, many tenant farmers stayed for much shorter periods. Often, it seems, agricultural labourers stayed longer in the village than the tenants.

Mention must also be made of the early 19th-century plans which were created for local taxation and administrative purposes, and can cover a whole parish.

Mention must also be made of the early 19th-century plans which were created for local taxation and administrative purposes, and can cover a whole parish.

There are many such plans for the London area, such as Thompson's 1804 map of St Pancras; but they exist elsewhere, too, especially following the Parochial Assessments Act of 1836 (a valuation for Poor Law purposes). The visually striking map of Bright Waltham (fig.16), produced in about 1840, covers the whole parish at a scale of 10 miles to the inch and, by means of a large reference table drawn on the actual map, details the holdings (with acreage) of every tenant, distinguishing between cottage and garden, workshop, orchard, meadow and coppice.

■ Locating the maps

Finding and accessing estate surveys for a particular location can be difficult. Local knowledge of who the principal landowners were in earlier centuries can help, but the fact that the one extant manuscript copy may be in the possession of a private landlord – who may not even have it properly catalogued – means it can be rather like looking for a needle in the proverbial haystack.

Nevertheless, many such maps have passed into the hands of record offices which have accumulated valuable collections. Amongst the numerous useful estate surveys held by Hampshire County Record Office, for instance, are maps and a book of reference for the Micheldever estate (owned by the Duke of Bedford) which gives detailed information on tenants (the maps are to be found at 92M95/f8/5/1-3 and the book of reference at 149M89/R2/144). Parish maps can also be difficult to find, though many libraries and other record offices now list them online. Camden Local Studies and Archives Centre has several parish maps listed, including J. Tompson's 1804 parish map of St Pancras which is quite large and covers the whole parish from Highgate to Bloomsbury, and comes with a terrier dated 1834.

FIGURE 16: *Parish map of Bright Waltham.* (Berkshire Record Office)

Enclosure Maps and Awards

THE 'TRADITIONAL' ENGLISH COUNTRYSIDE, WITH ITS PATCHWORK OF SMALL RECTANGULAR FIELDS BOUNDED BY FENCES, HEDGEROWS AND STRAIGHT COUNTRY ROADS, IS LARGELY THE CONSEQUENCE OF A PROCESS KNOWN AS 'ENCLOSURE' WHICH, IN MANY AREAS, REMOVED FROM THE LANDSCAPE THE ANCIENT LARGE OPEN ARABLE FIELDS, COMMONS, MEADOWS AND WASTELAND.

This re-making of the countryside was at its most intense in the later 18th and early 19th centuries. The processes involved often generated maps of landholding and land ownership, with accompanying written descriptions (known as 'awards'), which are invaluable to the family historian. They offer a visual and material resource which can help to identify and understand individual ancestors and/or the communities in which they lived. For the 18th century, in particular, an enclosure map may be the only large-scale map available.

For the 18th century, in particular, an enclosure map may be the only large-scale map available.

'Enclosure', in the sense that the term is used here, refers to the process of taking pieces of land into private ownership. Fences, hedges and other physical boundaries are simply physical markers of what was a key legal change: the removal of communal rights over land in favour of landownership 'in severalty' (the modern sense of ownership where the owner has full control over his land).

Enclosure itself was not a new development in the 18th century. A quarter of Berkshire, for example, was already enclosed by the year 1600. Piecemeal and larger-scale enclosure had, indeed, been going on since the Middle Ages. The actions of monastic and lay landowners, enclosing land for sheep farming in earlier

THE OPEN FIELD SYSTEM

Under the open field system, farmers cultivated their own strips of land spread across different fields, but were not free to decide what to grow and when to harvest. Such decisions were under communal control as, too, was the management of commons and wastes. Villagers, officially or unofficially, enjoyed certain customary rights of access and usage over such land, such as grazing animals on the commons or being able to collect firewood. In many places, enclosure was about the taking of these commons and wastes into private ownership and the abolition of such commoners' rights.

centuries, are well known. The famous statesman Thomas More, in a vitriolic attack on the perpetrators of such enclosures (in his book *Utopia* of 1516), declared that sheep had become 'so great devourers and so wild, that they eat up, and swallow down the very men themselves'.

In those cases, enclosure of the arable lands, commons, wastes and woodland took place as a formal or informal process, with the latter often leaving no paper trail. Formal agreements between the (principal) landowners of a village or locality, by their very nature, are more likely to have been recorded. However, the family historian is most likely to encounter documents which have resulted from enclosure by private Act of Parliament (or under the later series of General Acts of Parliament dating from 1801, 1836 and 1845). Although expensive and time-consuming – especially if the original bill provoked counter petitions – the use of private Acts of Parliament became a favoured means of enclosure in England from the later 18th century onwards and the process is known as 'parliamentary enclosure'. More than 4,000 private Acts were passed in the hundred years after 1750, with many more occurring under the later General Acts.

Parliamentary enclosure by private Act of Parliament was heavily concentrated in the 1760s and 1770s and, again, in the period 1790-1810 (when we were at war with the French and grain prices rose sharply). Agricultural improvers, like the well-known propagandist Arthur Young, condemned the existing agricultural system as inefficient and the opportunity to try out new crop and husbandry techniques was always an incentive for enclosure, whether the period concerned was one of high or low grain prices. Enclosure also provided many landholders with an opportunity to negotiate an end to tithes (payments in kind to the Church – see Chapter 6) which they found irksome.

Whilst estimates vary, during the parliamentary enclosure movement of the 18th and 19th centuries it is believed that at least a quarter of the cultivated acreage in England was enclosed. Although particularly associated with the division of large, open, arable fields, in fact, outside the arable Midlands belt, parliamentary enclosure was often about the use of commons and/or wastes (as was the case with Yorkshire). Of course, the process was patchy, even at the county level, with over 54% of Oxfordshire being enclosed by Act of Parliament, but less than 17% of Hampshire and below 1% of Kent. Some areas of the country, like Devon, Cornwall and the South-East were, indeed, little affected. In Wales, however, outside the Welsh Marches, parliamentary enclosure had a considerable impact, although the chronology was rather different.

In response to the obvious popularity of private enclosure acts (the progress of which can, with varying degrees of success, be followed in printed House of Commons' Journals), the government attempted to make the process easier. A series of General Acts led to the setting up of permanent Parliamentary Commissioners who could make parliamentary awards. The General Act of 1845 is worth highlighting for two reasons: nearly half of all Welsh parliamentary enclosures took place under this Act and the copies of all awards and maps made under the Act are stored at The National Archives.

Formal enclosure by Act of Parliament during this period means that there is a reasonable likelihood that the award, or some version of it, survives, usually in the county record office. However, the existence of an act (let alone a bill) does not mean that, ipso facto, an award was made. Where an 18th-century award is found, it often gives a better and more detailed description of plots than a 19th-century one. Those awards made before 1790 may be accompanied by a map, detailing all the allotments and their 'owners' (freehold and, perhaps,

Whilst estimates vary, during the parliamentary enclosure movement of the 18th and 19th centuries it is believed that at least a quarter of the cultivated acreage in England was enclosed.

USING ENCLOSURE MAPS AND AWARDS

What do they look like and how does one use them? Maps vary considerably in scale and size and, until the early 19th century, were usually on parchment. They will show plots with the names of allotees (those 'allotted' land) and either acreages or plot numbers. These correspond with entries in the written award document. Other details one can expect to find on a map are the public allotments (such as a gravel pit), roads and paths. Field names are also often given and the map may retain the names of former open fields. Helpfully, areas outside the newly-enclosed land may be shown, including those of old enclosure and local settlement.

copyhold), but awards after that date will usually do so.

The award document itself, often clearly written, can take the form of a bound book or of a number of single, rolled parchment sheets. As awards were local creations made by the Commissioner(s) appointed by the Act, their arrangement can vary, but the preamble will include reference to the prime movers of the Act and give the name of the Commissioner(s) charged with carrying out the enclosure. The main body of the document will consist of successive pages detailing the private allotments: the name of the allottee, the acreage (in imperial measurements) and the location, as well as, where relevant, the plot number as recorded on the map. The document will also detail private and public roads and public allotments (to be used, for example, for the upkeep of the poor).

As it was each landowner's responsibility to pay the costs of enclosing his lands, Commissioners were concerned about charges and their payment within a certain time frame. Rev. Thomas Lumley, owner of Acomb Rectory in Yorkshire, who was well compensated for giving up his tithes and customary rights under the Acomb and Holgate enclosure award of the 1770s, had the sizeable bill of £500 5s 1d! It was usual for incumbents such as the Reverend Lumley to agree to 'compensation', in the form of land, for the loss of tithe rights. Indeed the ending of tithes could be as important a motive for enclosure as agricultural improvement (see Chapter 6). Canny vicars often

FIGURE 17 (OVER): *Askham Richard Enclosure Award 1813:1821 map, award with plan (scale 5 chains to one inch). The map shows the whole township. (York City Archives)*

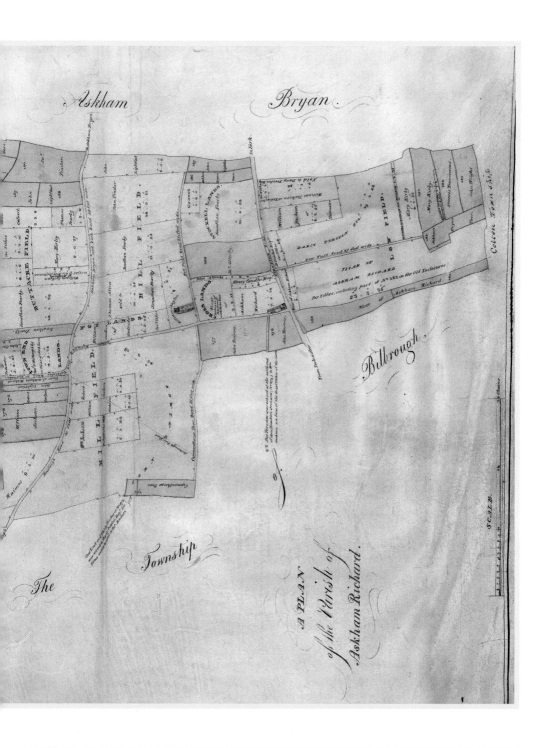

closes containing thirteen acres two roods and ten
perches bounded on all sides by old inclosed lands
of the said Robert Swann **And I order and**
direct that the said Robert Swann and the
owners for the time being of the said several closes
or parcels of land so awarded in exchange shall
make and for ever maintain such as ditches and
fences as have heretofore usually belonged to and been
maintained by the owners thereof for the time being
I do also allot appoint and award
unto the said Robert Swann **In exchange**
from the said William Jackson of Tadcaster as
hereinbefore mentioned **All those** two closes or parcels
of ground called Ox closes one of them containing four
acres one rood and twenty six perches and the
other containing five acres and twenty four perches
Which said closes lie together and
are bounded on the east by the Township of Askham

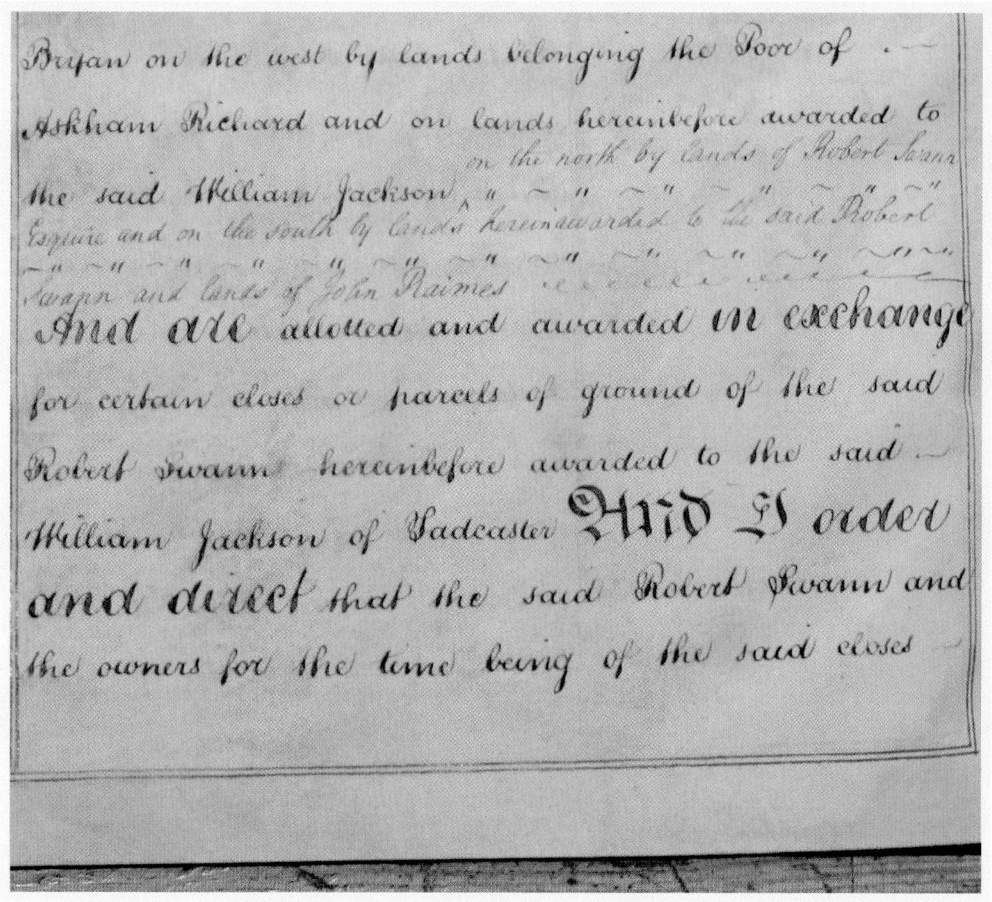

FIGURE 18: *Askham Richard Enclosure Award 1813:1821, page from the Award document. Robert Swann was keen to consolidate holdings through exchanges of land.* (York City Archives)

tried to hold on to valuable tithes, especially during wartime when commodity prices could be expected to rise.

Whilst incumbents, and the principal landowners affected by an award, might be awarded large acreages, allocations of just a few acres of land could equally be recorded. This should not be read as suggesting the landowner concerned was poor – many would in fact own property elsewhere, whether locally or further away. True 'cottagers', without title or unable to fund the changeover to enclosed farming, will be largely absent from the records. In the Shropshire manor of Ditton Priors, for example, only a very few cottagers received any land as compensation for the loss of commons and wastes. Some researchers may be surprised to find women holding allotments of land – and not always because of widowhood.

A VALUABLE SNAPSHOT

Taking the early 19th-century enclosure of Askham Richard (fig.17) as an example, we are offered a valuable snapshot of a rural community at a point in time. The map and award covers the whole township and took longer than the average to complete, no doubt partly because of the death of the first commissioner appointed to carry out the wishes of Parliament. The hand-coloured map shows plot/field boundaries – sometimes field names too – along with the owners' names and plot numbers. Roads and public allotments are included, as are the names of former open fields (such as Hill Field). The map also gives a clear view of the village and its buildings and refers to land exchanges which are further documented in the award itself (fig.18). Such exchanges – and the indication of a land sale – suggest enterprising landowners and a community in transition.

Where a thorough survey with a map – covering a whole or part of a village – was made, it was nothing less than a definitive statement of title to land (in the same way that tithe maps and schedules could be for a later time period).

Enclosure changed the mental map of villagers and had mixed economic benefits for the different layers of rural society. Communal management of agriculture, whereby key decisions were made in manorial courts, was replaced by individual holdings held in severalty where each farmer could act as he saw fit. Rights to the commons, meadow, wastes and woodland, which allowed even the poorest some cushion against economic misfortune, were destroyed. Those small landowners and cottagers who could not afford the costs associated with enclosure, or relied on commons to graze an animal or two and waste to gather winter fuel, found themselves either reliant on employment by wealthier neighbours or drifting into the expanding towns in search of a better life. Although minor roads created upon enclosure were often straightened versions of existing ones, the need to allow efficient access to holdings (as in Hessay, Yorkshire, in 1831) could lead to a road layout which altered the whole rhythm of everyday life.

Superimposing the enclosure map on the OS map immediately shows a remarkable degree of correspondence between the two.

■ Comparing a map with corroborative evidence

As with all sources, enclosure maps and documents have to be used with a measure of circumspection. The fact that the local community had so much at stake with an enclosure award, however, means that the map and award were likely to come in for close scrutiny, while landowners were concerned with both title to their land and its value.

Obvious features of the map can be checked against later OS maps and photographs. The Winnersh (Berkshire) enclosure process took an incredible 36 years, being completed in 1844. Much of the land was owned by rich landlords (including Jesus College, Oxford) and let to local farmers and other tenants. The map, showing the layout of fields and roads (fig.19), can be compared with the six-inch Ordnance Survey map of the same area, surveyed in 1871/72 and published in 1883 (fig.20), and even an aerial RAF photograph taken on 12th March 1945.

Superimposing the enclosure map on the OS map immediately shows a remarkable degree of correspondence between the two. Field shapes have largely survived, although there has been some amalgamation and consolidation. For example, field 328 on the enclosure award, listed as King Street Coppice, has survived in outline as King Street Gorse, despite being bisected by the railway line opened in 1849. Field 548, near the 'Rectory', and field 550, near Winnersh Grove, are almost identical on both, whereas others have been combined into larger fields (e.g. 552 and 553).

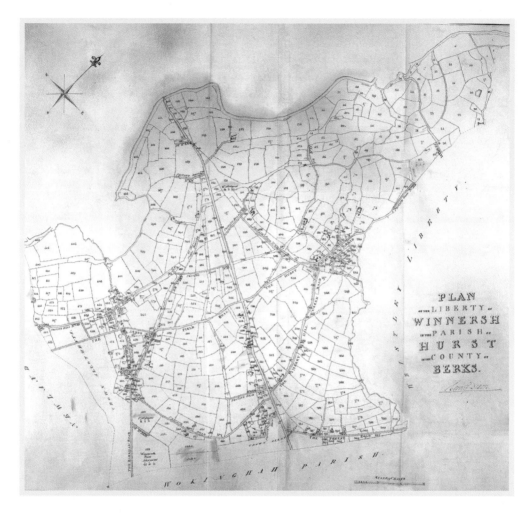

The field patterns on the OS map are in turn very similar to those shown on the aerial photograph. Over time of course there have been name changes to the roads. The road to the right of plot 580 was called Tylers Lane in the award but is now known as Sadlers Lane. Interestingly, the award shows that both the Sadler family and Tyler family once had houses along this lane. Plot 570 on the map, described as 'the Rectory', was in fact a private house by 1871/2 although the OS map fails to record this change of use. On the photograph, the land belonging to the Rectory – marked as Glebe on the OS map – can be clearly

FIGURE 19: *Winnersh Enclosure Map of 1843 (enrolled in 1844). Both map and award are available online at www.berkshirenclosure. org.uk. (Berkshire Record Office)*

*The content
of enclosure
awards can be
checked against
a range of more
contemporary
sources, including
literary ones,
though omissions
and defects can
be hard to detect.*

seen, and at the top right of this land there is a pond, known at the time of the photograph as Wheelers Pond. This is marked on the OS map and on the enclosure map (where it is shown as a Public Watering Place).

The content of enclosure awards can be checked against a range of more contemporary sources, including literary ones, though omissions and defects can be hard to detect. Owners' names present particular problems in the absence of a full set of deeds to local properties. Frequently an owner died whilst the enclosure process was taking place and consequently the new owner's name may not be given, or the name(s) recorded may actually refer to executors of his will. There is also the annoying fact that many holdings changed hands shortly after enclosure. Only Yorkshire and Middlesex have registers of deeds, which make it easier to track such market activity.

The exact status of the landowners may also be impossible to determine, either because of missing information or due to the fact that awards do not often cover a whole parish or village. Very small holdings can be listed but a small allotment does not equate to a minor landholder unless one is certain that no land is held elsewhere. There is also the problem that with later 19th-century awards descriptions can be very brief, limiting the usefulness of enclosure material even when a map is present. By their very nature enclosure awards are unlikely to record information about the poorer inhabitants of villages.

*Manorial records
(surveys, rentals
and court
records) can be
useful as a form
of corroborative
evidence of
landholdings*

Manorial records (surveys, rentals and court records) can be useful as a form of corroborative evidence of landholdings. Unfortunately, a manorial court may represent only a small part of a village or, conversely, several villages! Court Baron records give information on the holders of copyhold land – but are a difficult source to interpret – whilst Court Leet records deal with day-to-day issues and petty trangressions of community law. Court Leet records do, at least, have some potential to reach deep down inside the rural community.

Enclosure could bring great hardship to people living at or just above the poverty line. Popular opposition against enclosure was rare, but judicial records will take notice of individual 'criminals' brave enough to invade newly enclosed land – although, in legal speak, the charge was often 'forcible entry'. Such records

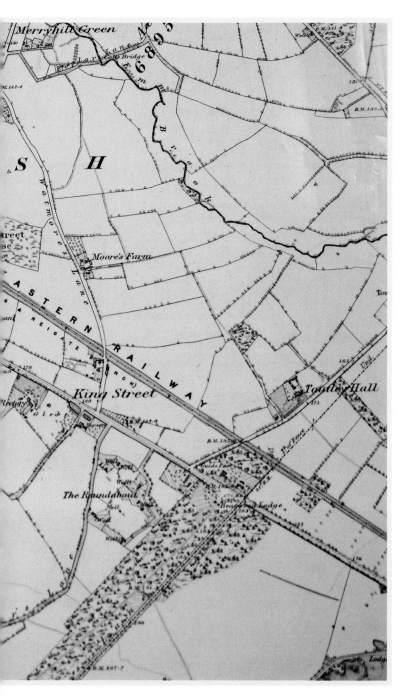

FIGURE 20: *Winnersh, taken from the OS Berkshire six inch map sheet 38 surveyed in 1871-2 and 1877. It was engraved in 1881 and published in 1883.*

include those of Quarter Sessions, located at the county record office and a rich source of local information. Justices of the Peace did not just concern themselves with crime and punishment and one can hope to find here, for example, settlement dispositions under the Poor Law which often give biographical details on lowly members of the community. Records in connection with the Old Poor Law are often plentiful in county record offices and under-used. In particular, the accounts of local overseers list disbursements of relief to the poor which throw light on individuals and, perhaps, families too. In Essex and other record offices, pauper letters can be located in which we hear the authentic voice of the poor as they plead for relief or seek to avoid removal from the parish in which they are living.

Example: **Levisham, North Yorkshire**

How enclosure records can be used successfully, in conjunction with other records, to build up a profile of a village and its inhabitants is best illustrated by an example. Levisham is a small village, 30 miles from York, on the edge of the North Yorks Moors. It is fortunate to have an 18th-century enclosure award (made by agreement), but the lack of any map would appear a serious drawback, especially as there is the complication of pre-existing 'old enclosures' and private 'closes' (around the village periphery) to contend with. Fortunately, unlike in many areas where there is either an enclosure award or a tithe award but not both, the existence of an 1848 tithe map allows the individual allocations mentioned in the 1770 award document to be plotted successfully on to it with only minor discrepancies. The map (fig.21) gives a whole new dimension to the study and also shows clearly that Levisham, like some other villages in the Vale of Pickering, was apparently a 12th-century planned village! It is also instructive to realize when driving through the village that these lanes date from the enclosure award, as do many of the fields that can be viewed over the top of substantial dry stone walls and hedges.

'An enclosure award gives a complete survey of the land and its ownership.' (Betty Halse, Levisham local historian – see Sources for Further Research on page 122)

The Levisham award of 1770 was the outcome of an agreement between the principal inhabitants, including the Rector, Isaac Wykes, who, like many other incumbents across the country, was generously rewarded with land for the loss of most of his tithe rights. No doubt, the desire of villagers to remove tithes was a motive behind the enclosure award here as it was in other places. The award details how the three arable fields in the village, amounting to 525 acres, were divided up.

As with other enclosures, Commissioners surveyed the area first and tried to take account of the quality of the land in arriving at their judgments. Decisions as to allocations were only made after consultation with those affected. The prime movers behind the enclosure agreement were the principal gainers too. Isaac Wykes, already referred to, received an allotment amounting to nearly 18% of the total. Robert Harding, who did not live in the village, got about the same amount, whilst Ralph Graystock of Pickering received only a little less. Perhaps surprisingly, William Poad, Lord of the Manor, had a holding of only about 10% of the total.

'With maps and schedules, a great deal can be... worked out about the structure of the village... especially when linked with Parish Registers and Census returns.' (Betty Halse)

The general picture that emerges, however, is of a relatively poor farming community practising, in the main, subsistence agriculture. The probate inventory of one of the Poad family for 1734, although likely to be only a partial version of the actual situation, suggests, at best, a relatively modest set of possessions. The fact that under post-enclosure market conditions core (long-standing) families were largely to become a thing of the past in the village is suggestive of the struggle that 'subsistence' farmers faced.

The Levisham study is particularly noteworthy because it shows the value of bringing together as many sources as can be found. Although the accounts of the overseers of the poor seem to have been lost, there is at least a Pauper Book for the early 19th century. This throws light on the attitudes of the Levisham community towards its poorer inhabitants and shows how family fortunes could change. Priscilla Jackson, widow and daughter of the once significant Adamson family – at least earlier church terriers suggest as much – is regularly listed as receiving various forms of sustained poor relief. The parish registers and the remarkable Yorkshire Register of Deeds from 1763 (in the North Yorkshire County Record Office) make up for some of the other source gaps.

Using these sources, detailed profiles have been built up for many of the villagers and their families. It is even possible,

FIGURE 21: *Levisham Enclosure Map. (Courtesy of Betty Halse)*

ENCLOSURE AWARD
1770

Transposed onto 1848
Tithe Map

with admittedly a degree of conjecture, to gain an insight into attitudes and personalities. James Read, yeoman, who figures in the enclosure award, came from one of the core families in the village. The Read family had been in Levisham since the 16th century, and wills show the family had some substance. James Read was also a collector of the Land Tax in 1788. Ralph Greystoke, with his rather stylish signature, was a 'go-getter' around the village and perhaps should be regarded as an entrepreneur. Robert Harding, 'gentleman', also a principal mover of the award, seems to have been of a similar character and to have come to the village not long before enclosure, where he saw opportunities for post-enclosure farming. The Harding family was well-established in the Pickering area, and in The National Archives there are papers referring to law suits involving a William Harding over the enclosure of common lands.

The archivist of the county record office concerned will know where local awards are.

The Poads, too, were a long-established family in the village. William Poad, Lord of the Manor, unfortunately died shortly after the enclosure and his son sold the land and title to an outsider. Most of the villagers, however, were only subsistence farmers – certainly at the time of the enclosure award. Unfortunately, enclosure awards do not, on the whole, concern themselves with buildings – except to identify plots – but the fact that few pre-19th-century houses exist in the village points to the relative poverty of inhabitants in the earlier period.

■ Locating the maps

Finding aids have greatly improved in recent years and there are reference books which have removed most of the donkey work. The archivist of the county record office concerned will know where local awards are. There can be more than one copy of an award since originally one was placed in the parish chest and another, quite often, lodged with the Clerk of the Peace to the County. Of course, family historians must be prepared to find that there may well be no award covering a particular parish or village. Frustration can arise, too, when an award was made but the document has been 'lost' (though a copy may still actually exist somewhere in private hands). Sometimes, regrettably, only a poor or partial copy of an award or map remains.

How do you determine whether or not there is an enclosure award/map for your area? An excellent resource is Roger. J. P. Kain, John Chapman, and Richard R. Oliver, *The Enclosure Maps of England and Wales, 1595-1918: A Cartographic Analysis and Electronic Catalogue* (Cambridge University Press, 2004). The electronic web catalogue listing all known maps that accompanies this book is available at http://hds.essex.ac.uk/em/index.html.

The National Archives may have some records but it is best to consult the local record office first. Record offices are increasingly making it easier to search their holdings online. The Berkshire Record Office has produced a superb online feature on enclosures, complete with enclosure map! For those readers seeking more information on the enclosure process itself, M. E. Turner's *Enclosures in Britain 1750-1830* (London, 1984) is well worth consulting. For manorial records, consult the National Archives' Manorial Records Register (for some areas now searchable online at http://www.nationalarchives.gov.uk/mdr).

5

Town Maps

FAMILY HISTORIANS WHO HAVE CONSULTED THE LARGE-SCALE ORDNANCE SURVEY TOWN MAPS OF THE SECOND HALF OF THE 19TH CENTURY WILL BE AWARE OF THEIR IMMENSE DETAIL. MOST TOWNS WITH A POPULATION OF OVER 4,000 (AT THE TIME OF A SURVEY) WERE MAPPED AT LEAST ONCE BY THE ORDNANCE SURVEY AT THE VERY USEFUL 1:500 SCALE.

Such maps, showing as they do external features of buildings and even divisions within tenements, are a particularly useful resource. In the case of York, for instance, the late 19th-century map extends to 72 sheets and uses colour for buildings. It is possible to identify individual properties, view the layouts of buildings and streets and find street names that may have long since vanished. At the largest scales, it is even possible to examine architectural details which can have social significance and see such minute features of the everyday landscape as lamp posts and manhole covers. In conjunction with censuses, directories and rate books, it is possible to link households with where they lived and, in so doing, determine to some extent how they lived.

OS maps are not the only large-scale maps of towns to be found.

As we have already discovered, however, OS maps are not the only large-scale maps of towns to be found. County map-makers, such as Speed and, later, Donn, inserted town plans on their county maps – sometimes, as is the case with Donn's maps of Exeter and the Plymouth area, the town maps are on a larger scale than the county maps themselves. Estate owners, too, could decide to have towns mapped in detail. For the second half of the 19th century there are, for some of the larger urban areas in particular, maps produced by local Boards of Health (with or without the assistance of OS map-makers) and 'social' or 'poverty' maps such as those of Charles Booth and Goad.

Goad Maps

The Goad maps (produced by the firm of Chas E. Goad Ltd for fire insurance purposes from 1886 until the 1960s) have commercial buildings as their focus – which they mapped in incredible detail down to the level of individual skylights, which were coloured blue; nevertheless, as part of its risk assessment, the Goad company also mapped nearby residential areas. Produced usually at a scale of 40 inches to a mile and updated, at least in part, every half dozen years, they cover parts of the urban areas of many of our larger towns and cities, including Birmingham, Cardiff, Leeds, Manchester and Southampton. Tenements, pubs, shops and houses are distinguished and house numbers marked. Since the Post Office changed street numbering in the early 20th century, Goad maps can help (along with the Valuation Office Survey, see Chapter 7) to resolve confusion when seeking to positively identify particular properties.

Although there are some fire insurance town plans dating from the 18th century, the Goad plans are more plentiful.

Often a series of Goad maps for an area can be found in fairly local record offices. Camden Local Studies and Archive Centre, for instance, has Goad maps from as early as 1886 and Bath Central Library has a number of Goad maps dating from 1902 to at least the 1930s. The 1902 Goad map of Bath (fig.22) comes from a set of nine coloured maps (plus a 'key' map). Each property is identified by occupier type and business name, or use if a commercial property. House numbers are given as appropriate.

Comparing the Goad map for the Somerset Street area of the city of Bath with contemporary sources such as the census for 1901 and directories, we are able to locate individuals and build up a picture of what was a lower working class area, but one where some of the unskilled were evidently trying to better themselves by putting their sons to a trade. Only one business owner lived on the street, and she was a widow living above the business.

Although there are some fire insurance town plans dating from the 18th century, the Goad plans are much more plentiful. The fact that frequent revisions to the plans were carried out can be very useful, although updates of areas may simply take the annoying form of superimposing additions over existing details – thereby obscuring the earlier information.

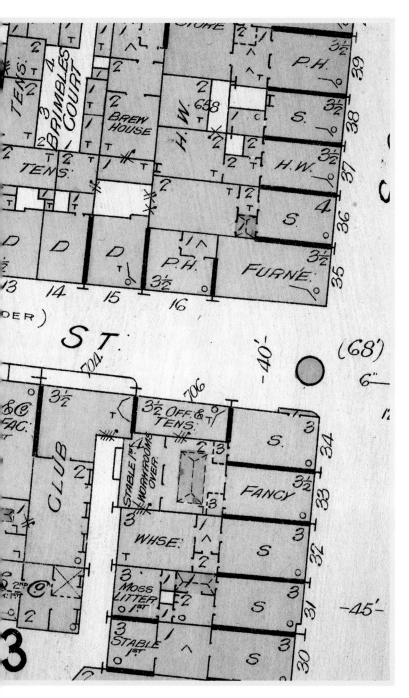

FIGURE 22: *Goad map 1902, showing the Somerset Street area of Bath. Notice that TENS = tenements. (www.bathintime.co.uk – Images of Bath Online)*

■ 'Social' maps

Mention must be made of mid 19th- and later 19th-century thematic maps showing the incidence of disease, poverty or drinking establishments. Cholera, as a water-borne disease which could affect rich as well as poor, was of particular concern. Although the medical practitioner most closely identified with the cholera issue is the famous John Snow, who was a doctor working in mid 19th-century London, Dr Thomas Shapter produced a cholera map for Exeter in the early 1830s 'shewing the localities where the deaths caused by Pestilential Cholera' had occurred (fig.23).

Most 'social' maps do not have any great value for the family historian, but Charles Booth's social class maps of London in the 1890s, produced in connection with his study of poverty in the capital, are an exception. Booth's work is of particular significance because of the additional data he collected in the later 1880s on households in the East End to go with his 'poverty

Most 'social' maps do not have any great value for the family historian, but Charles Booth's social class maps of London in the 1890s, produced in connection with his study of poverty in the capital, are an exception.

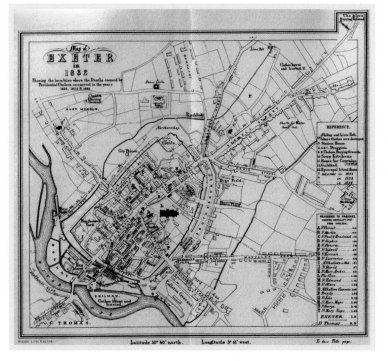

FIGURE 23: *Dr Thomas Shapter's Cholera Map is taken from his book* History of the Cholera in Exeter in 1832 *which was published in 1849. The single red lines indicate deaths in 1832, the crossed lines deaths in 1833 and the dots deaths in 1834.*

map' (fig.24). Contained in 50 handwritten notebooks is the household information he collected with the help of London school attendance officers.

Although family names are not given, addresses are and, under suitable column headings, the occupation of household heads (male and female), the rents payable, the number of children (especially of school age) and some snippets of social commentary at street and even household level are recorded. The picture that emerges in poorer areas is of inhabitants, often immigrants, struggling with poverty and exploitation. Many such individuals gained employment in the sweated trades.

Streets in Whitechapel, for instance, associated with the Ripper murders of the period, are characterized as places of cheap lodging houses, prostitution and shifting populations, where the inhabitants come from the lowest social classes. Of Grace Alley, Booth writes it is 'a queer place – low class of people'. In the case of Flower Street, which was allegedly the street in which Jack the Ripper actually lived, Booth refers to the cheap lodging houses and 'the houses let out in small furnished rooms ... used mostly by prostitutes'. He refers, here, too, to a 'shifting' population 'who are all of the very lowest class'. Thawl Street is given a similarly negative description, yet at No.18 is a poor family who are said to be 'fairly decent'. Used with the census and other sources, the map and accompanying comments are not without value for those looking at East End communities.

The 13th-century Mappa Mundi world map, on display at Hereford, may be famous but maps with any resemblance to reality were almost unknown until early modern times.

Town Plans

Yet what of actual plans for London and other towns in earlier periods when mapping and production techniques were more primitive?

As with other kinds of maps, the earliest useful maps date from the Elizabethan period when, for example, coastal towns like Portsmouth and Dover could be covered as part of a wider exercise in mapping strategic harbours and coastal defences.

The 13th-century Mappa Mundi world map, on display at Hereford, may be famous but maps with any resemblance to reality were almost unknown until early modern times. Medieval town maps are not only scarce but were simply generic or symbolic constructions. Robert Ricart's 1480 bird's-eye view of

FIGURE 24: *Charles Booth's 'Map Descriptive of London Poverty' 1898-9, Sheet 5, East Central District. A map of his study of London poverty appeared as early as 1891. Booth used different colours for each street to reflect social class. The spectrum of seven colours included black (for the lowest, often semi-criminal, class); two shades of blue (for the working class poor); and red (for the middle class).* (Courtesy London School of Economics)

the central part of Bristol, for instance, does at least have some links with reality but fails to record many of the buildings then certainly present in the city. 'Bird's-eye', or perspective views, rather than the more familiar ground plan, were popularized by Elizabethan map-makers and continued to have a market in fashionable cities like Bath and York right up to the 19th century – Whittock's 1858 view of York is both spectacular and generally accurate, although his earlier view of Oxford tactfully hid from view (by means of a shadow) a notoriously rough area of the city known as St Ebbe's!

Elizabethan town maps, as one would expect, vary greatly in quality and accuracy and like many later ones were more concerned to highlight prominent buildings than to record ordinary dwellings. Aga's Oxford map of 1577-88 is large scale but poorly executed, in contrast to John Hammond's map of Cambridge of 1592. William Smith's 1568 map of Bristol, despite defects of scale, was seen as worthy of inclusion in both G. Braun and F. Hogenberg's *Civitates Orbis Terrarum* world atlas of towns and Speed's *Theatre of the Empire of Great Britaine* (1611-12).

If Elizabethan map-makers made important contributions to the early mapping of towns, Speed's work, with its bird's-eye town plans inserted on county maps, was the real landmark in the history of town mapping. Many of the towns were surveyed for the first time and the majority of the 73 maps included were by Speed himself who was keen to produce accurate plans based on actual observation. Nevertheless, Speed's maps were often hurriedly surveyed leading to errors (not least in place-names) and, as was often the case, buildings could be stylized rather than accurately depicted. Speed's scale map of 'Newe:castle', one of two town maps inserted on his map of Northumberland (the other was Berwick), could well be his own work. Usefully, it shows urban expansion northwards from the river and has a key for important buildings, but it is not a full and accurate portrayal of all existing settlement there at that time.

Despite the success of Speed's *Theatre*, it was the 1666 Fire of London which did more to spur on map-makers to fresh efforts. Notable maps of the period include John Ogilby and William Morgan's 1677 map of the rebuilt capital on 21 sheets,

If Elizabethan map-makers made important contributions to the early mapping of towns, Speed's work, with its bird's-eye town plans inserted on county maps, was the real landmark in the history of town mapping.

It was the 1666 Fire of London which did more to spur on map-makers to fresh efforts.

at a scale of 100 ft to an inch. Ogilby also produced a map of Ipswich at the same scale in 1674 which gives house plots and the names of some owners. Whilst maps from this period often drew street plans reliably, it is unfortunately the case that map-making was concentrated on towns that were prosperous and whose inhabitants, out of perceived necessity or civic pride, were able and willing to fund new projects.

During the 18th century, town maps increased markedly in volume and accuracy. As with a number of other early 18th-century maps, Stukeley's 1723 map of Bath combined the new style of mapping – plan form – with the showing of certain important buildings in elevation (Bath Abbey, other churches and the city walls and gates). When maps proclaimed that they were based on new surveys, this was more likely than previously to be the case. John Wood's 1735 map of Bath is original; he certainly did not copy Stukeley's map and may never have even viewed it. Unlike the Elizabethan map by Saville and the late 17th-century one by Gilmore (fig.25) – which used the bird's-eye view – Wood's map of Bath was completely in plan form.

Maps of the period, even well produced ones, continued to suffer from defects which were often partly the product of surveying techniques.

Maps of the period, even well produced ones, continued to suffer from defects which were often partly the product of surveying techniques. There is often no attempt to indicate boundaries between properties or the footprint of individual buildings (except public ones). Town blocks are indicated with shaded areas between streets, contrasting with special treatment for public buildings, such as churches, which are shown in more convincing plan. Backyards and gardens, which the surveyor had neither the ability nor resources to access, are consequently obscured. Both Rocque, in his map of London, Westminster and Southwark (1746), and Donn, in his map of Exeter (1765), show town properties in this way. In Donn's plan of Stoke Town and Plymouth Dock we see the terrace of naval officers' houses, their chapel and some smaller buildings in the vicinity in plan, in contrast to the unconvincingly regular blocks of private properties.

Map-makers not only found public buildings easier to inspect and therefore map, they also quite naturally tended to show more concern for what was open to public scrutiny and was likely to appeal to subscribers. Where private garden plans are

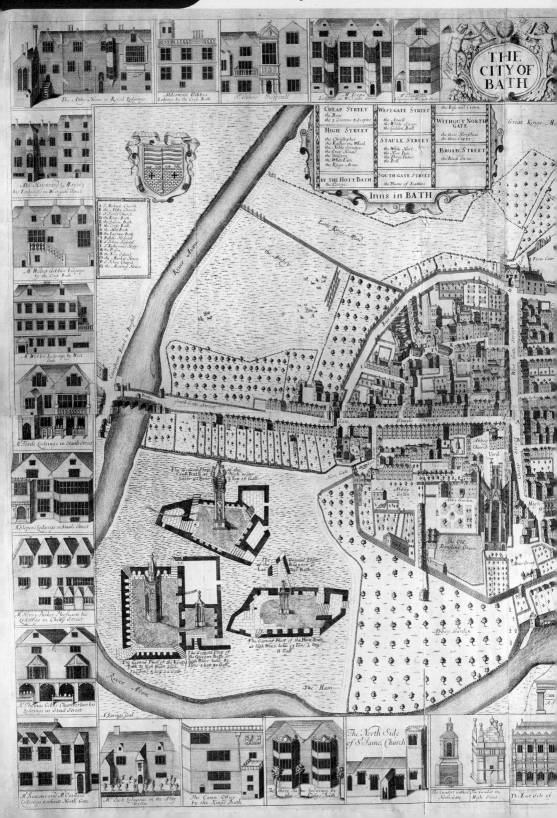

THE
CITY OF
BATH

The Abby House or Royal Lodgings

Alderman Gibbs Lodgings by the Cross Bath

S.t Johns Hospitall

M.r Loops Lodgings in Westgate Street

Mr. Reynard Mayor his Lodgings in Westgate Street

Mr. Walter Gibbs Lodgings by the Cross Bath

Mr. Webbs Lodgings by West Gate

Mr. Fords Lodgings in Staull Street

Mr. Slopers Lodgings in Stauls Street

Mr. Henry Parker Phisecion his Lodgings in Cheap Street

Mr. Thomas Gibbs Chamberline his Lodgings in Staul Street

River Avon

South Gate Street

River Avon

Causham Road to Bristol

The Ham

I. Savage Sculp

Mr. Beacons and Mr. Cranses Lodgings without North Gate

Mr. Earls Lodgings in the Abby Green

The Cann Office by the Kings Bath

The three Tuns Lodgings by the Kings Bath

The North Side of S.t James Church

The Cundict withoot North Gate

The Cundict in High Street

The East Side of

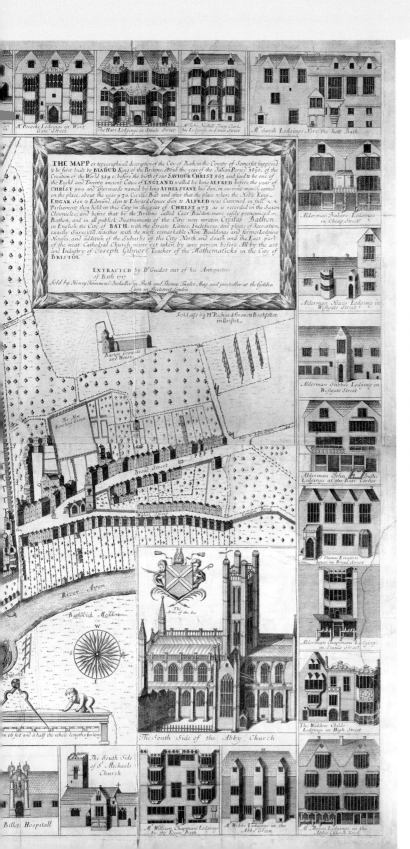

FIGURE 25: *Gilmore's map of Bath 1696, extracted by Dr Guidot out of his* Antiquities of Bath, 1717. *The city is still at this point largely confined within its walls.* (www.bathintime.co.uk – Images of Bath Online)

shown, such as the Royal Crescent in the 1771 map of Bath by booksellers Frederick and Taylor, they can appear convincing, but it may be that the surveyor is simply indicating formal gardens. The depiction of somewhere like Spring Gardens, on the other hand, might be more accurate because these were open to the public (for a fee!).

Inaccuracies in maps of the period also have other less obvious causes. Town development, proposed or real, created particular problems. Many map-makers were not as scrupulous as Frederick and Taylor (later Taylor and Meyler), who issued a series of maps, each time bringing the information up to date. When they published 'A New Plan of the City of Bath with the

WOOD'S MAP OF BATH

Maps of places like Bath, London and Oxford which record schemes for development or improvement need to be checked against later maps and even by on-the-spot footwork to see if such schemes ever materialised. Too many maps of the period show buildings and other developments that were planned, but not actually built. Wood's map of Bath is a good example. The architect hoped to build a circular hospital on land west of the city walls and this proposed building appears on his map. He was thwarted and the General Hospital (later the Mineral Water Hospital) was built in more conventional plan on a different site. In contrast, his plan for the central garden of Queen Square, which he depicted in bold and confident detail (with dark shading), was carried out and can be confirmed by later plans including those of Frederick and Taylor.

Additional Buildings to the present time 1783', it was largely copied from the 1771 map, but showed Rivers Street as built-up rather than, as in the earlier map, a proposal.

It was natural that wealthy centres were more frequently mapped than towns like Totnes in Devon and other quiet backwaters. York was at one time the so-called 'Capital of the North' and places like Bristol and Norwich had a long and important history. Family historians tracing ancestors in such locations are fortunate and may be able to consult a series of worthwhile maps.

One of the most impressive 18th-century attempts to produce a new and accurate survey, which was then kept up-to-date in successive editions, was Richard Horwood's 1798 map of London (fig.26). Horwood, who had some previous experience as an estate surveyor, set out to produce the first detailed map

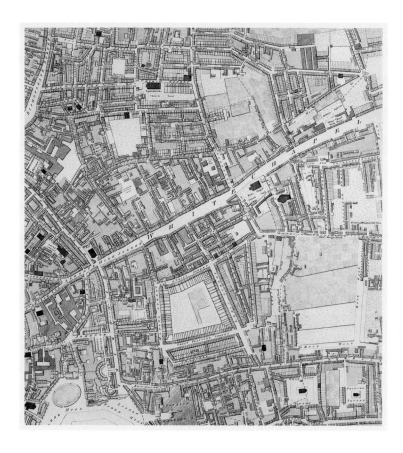

FIGURE 26: *Richard Horwood's map of London, 1798, sheet F2. The Whitechapel area shown can be compared with the Booth map one hundred years later.* (Courtesy Motco Enterprises Ltd)

Apart from the obvious exception of London, towns that may be of second rank today could have been of much greater importance in the past as county towns, ports or social centres.

of London since John Rocque's creditable effort some 50 years previously. In a nine-year odyssey, and despite both financial problems and deteriorating health, he attempted to map every house, business, court and alley and to give every house its actual number (where it had one). The result was a map of 32 sheets – the largest ever printed in Britain. Despite the defects (he failed to map every house, the back gardens of many properties were impossible to survey and parish boundaries were left incomplete), the survey was not to be superseded in terms of detail and quality until the arrival of the large-scale OS maps of the city. Although Horwood lived long enough to survey Liverpool, it was left to the publisher Faden to keep the map updated as London developed rapidly in the early 19th century – something, in this case, he tried to do quite meticulously. Family historians are left with a valuable resource, complete with street index.

For Bristol, there are the maps of Millerd (1673), Rocque (1742) and Benjamin Donn (1773). Millerd, although a mercer and not a professional map-maker, used his local knowledge to good effect to produce his bird's-eye view of the city.

Exeter, too, has a series of maps to choose from, although many of the maps published were derivatives of earlier ones. Hooker's landmark map of Exeter (1587), typically Tudor in its use of the bird's-eye view, was one of the first published for a provincial town. It was the basis for maps of Exeter for well over a century until Joseph Coles' 1709 survey, which was actually produced in the town. John Rocque's *Plan de la ville et faubourgs d'Exeter*, published in 1744 and printed on two copperplates, was the most accurate plan up to that date. It seems probable that Donn's 1765 map of the city (inserted on his county Map of Devon) was derived from it. Charles Tozer's plan of the city and suburbs of Exeter, which appeared in 1793, is also very much in the tradition of Rocque.

Sadly, in all too many cases, even when a map is known to exist from a secondary source (modern or old), it can be time-consuming to trace and access it.

Cities of great importance now, such as Manchester, may have been inconspicuous settlements for much of their history. Although Manchester began to be mapped before William Green's 60 yards to an inch plan of Manchester and Salford (1787-97), this quality map was a clear statement of the town's increasing affluence and industrial significance. It clearly shows not only prominent buildings, but also the back-to-back housing being created for the growing army of workers that such a 'showpiece' of the Industrial Revolution needed.

Sadly, in all too many cases, even when a map is known to exist from a secondary source (modern or old), it can be time-consuming to trace and access it. John Wood, a reputable Scottish surveyor whose work has already been referred to, produced maps of Exeter (1840), Bideford (1842) and Barnstaple (1843) at a time when he appears to have been based in Exeter itself. These maps show the built-up areas in great detail and the Exeter one can be used, not only with the 1841 census, but also alongside an almost contemporary valuation of houses and lands (by Rowe, Cooper and Hooper). Wood's maps were printed but those of the West Country towns, at least, are rare. The only original print of his Barnstaple map, which was produced for the Bridge Trust and is known to be extremely accurate, is in the Devon Record Office in Exeter where it is rolled up with the Barnstaple parish tithe map. A reduced quality tracing of it was made some years ago and published. The Westcountry Studies Library has only a photocopy of Wood's Bideford map, although a reproduction of the original map (believed to be held by North Devon Athenaeum) has been published by the Minerva Gallery, but is sadly out of print. The situation regarding Wood's Exeter map is far worse. The map is, as one would expect, to be found in the Devon County Record Office but is now in such a state of 'extreme fragility', according to the archivist, that it can neither be consulted nor photographed!

■ Locating the maps

Searching for town maps can be frustrating as well as rewarding, although websites such as Bath-in-Time (run in conjunction with Bath Central Library) are a delightful source for any researcher. It is, first of all, worth checking with a local record office or historical society that they have not re-published a map in their possession. Donn's map of Devon, which contains his Exeter and Plymouth plans, was published in 1965.

Although there are publications available about the Charles Booth's survey, it is worthwhile visiting the London School of Economics which has reproduction maps for sale. Charles Booth's research can also be explored online at http://booth.lse.ac.uk (run by the London School of Economics).

For information on which towns Goad maps cover, the reader should consult Chapter 15 of David T. Hawkings, *Fire Insurance Records for Family and Local Historians 1696 to 1920* (London, 2003). Although some Goad maps are to be found in The National Archives and other London collections, it is recommended to approach the relevant local record office first.

Harry Margary has published a reproduction of the Horwood map under the title *The A to Z of Regency London* (London Topographical Society, 1985).

J. West, *Town Records* (Chichester, 1983), lists English and Welsh town plans c.1600-1900.

6

Tithe Maps and Awards

Tithe maps — mostly dating from the later 1830s and early 1840s — are, for many parishes, the first large-scale maps available and are a key source in tracing ancestors back to the early Victorian period. Nearly half of all tithe maps have a scale of 20 or more miles to the inch, whilst those for some towns are on an even larger scale!

Two out of every three parishes in England and Wales, on average, were mapped in this way. Used in conjunction with the accompanying written schedule (known as the 'apportionment') and other sources like the 1841 census or the earlier Land Tax assessments, tithe maps can be the means of identifying individual houses, farms and premises, along with their owners and occupiers. Knowing the names of landowners in a parish also allows estate maps to be searched for. Parish and township boundaries are generally included, although place-names are not.

For England and Wales, tithe maps and accompanying apportionment schedules were made as a result of the Tithe Commutation Act of 1836 which substituted money payments for the payments in kind on yearly agricultural produce made to the church and other lay 'improprietors'. Intended for the upkeep of the local church and its clergyman, tithes had long been resented and were abolished in 1836 against a background of agricultural difficulties (including recent popular unrest) and the rise of religious nonconformity. The process of commutation had already been put in motion in Ireland by an Act of 1823, whilst Scotland, although having 'teinds', was not included.

The new (tithe) survey of England and Wales was under the ultimate control of three Tithe Commissioners in London with

Assistant Commissioners managing the process locally. The intention was to determine, clearly, what payments were due on each plot of land. Helpfully, the tithe districts, created in order to conduct the survey, frequently corresponded to existing parishes and townships

For many parishes and areas without estate or enclosure maps, the tithe maps are the most detailed maps of a location available prior to the appearance of the large-scale OS maps. Unlike enclosure awards (see Chapter 4), tithe awards give the names of occupiers of land as well as the owners. Unfortunately, it is often still the case that tithe maps and schedules may not exist for the particular area a family historian is interested in! Cornwall, Devon and Wales faired well in terms of overall coverage, but the Midlands did not. Almost a third of Buckinghamshire parishes have no such awards. Parishes responsible for relatively small parcels of tithable land frequently tried to sidestep the process because of the cost; whilst, in a particular location, tithes could already be in the hands of a single landowner (as was the case with North Stoke, Sussex) or have been extinguished as part of earlier enclosure agreements. In many parishes the tithable area only covers a small part of a parish anyway – as is the case with the village of Thorpe in Surrey. Nevertheless, the maps and apportionments of tithable land, where they exist, provide detailed information on landownership, occupancy and land use.

For many parishes and areas without estate or enclosure maps, the tithe maps are the most detailed maps of a location available prior to the appearance of the large-scale OS maps.

The tithe maps vary considerably in terms of content. Fields and parcels of land and various boundaries (including the tithe district boundary) are necessarily given centre stage, although it is usual to depict buildings, the major and minor routes (including rail), water features, gardens (including market gardens), orchards, parks and woods. Often the map will show (for rural areas anyway) the location of virtually every kind of building, including churches, industrial premises, inns, houses, cottages, stables and barns. Houses may be shown in red and outbuildings and other buildings in black or grey.

Tithe maps vary considerably in terms of content.

Each plot on the map has a number which can be related to the accompanying apportionment schedule, which lists landowners alphabetically by surname. The schedule, usually in manuscript, uses standard headings to record the plot number, the names of both owner and occupier, the name and description of the holding, the state of cultivation (generally in terms of whether the land was arable or pasture), the acreage, the (all-important) rent charge payable and 'remarks'. Since fields were the primary focus, the description of a plot often consists of a field name, although other entries frequently given include 'house and garden'. In the case of the Llandudno schedule of 1846, a number of plots near the village centre are collectively termed 'Poor cottages etc'.

Originally, tithe maps were intended to be at the large-scale of 3 chains to an inch (1:2,376) and of a high standard, but landlords, who had to pay for the survey, resented the cost implications and often preferred to let surveyors use existing estate and other local maps where possible. The result was, as might be expected, maps of different scales and reliability, although they are nearly always large scale affairs. Equally, the quality varied from landowner to landowner, but some whole areas, like Kent, nevertheless gained a reputation for high quality maps.

Besides the maps and schedules, it can be worth consulting the tithe files. These may contain descriptions of a place and its inhabitants (sometimes quite unflattering) and, where there was a case of disputed tithe, particular individuals in a parish can be referred to.

Using the tithe awards with a range of contemporary sources (including the 1841 and 1851 censuses) and field-work, communities and the lives of their inhabitants can be reconstructed in some detail. The awards can often, too, be a way of understanding how a community has developed or reacted to change. Llandudno, for instance, is unusual in having tithe and enclosure

'FIRST CLASS' MAPS

Maps that met the approval of the Tithe Commissioners in charge of the survey were sealed as 'first class' and were taken to be suitable for use in legal cases. Such first class maps account for only around 15% of all those produced. So-called 'second class' maps can, in fact, be surprisingly accurate and may also be at the scale demanded of first class maps. Yet there are many which are composite creations, based on maps of uncertain quality and provenance, or which amount to little more than the perfunctory overlaying of details on a one inch OS map (or even the drawing of a rough sketch). Maps that show a good deal about land use or give plenty of information on field names may be based on an earlier survey although this is by no means certain. Tithe surveyors were always far more concerned with acreages and rental values than recording land use or general details about the landscape.

awards completed within a year or so of each other (1846 and 1847 respectively). The timing, though, was not one of pure coincidence. The local landowner was busy developing the town as a seaside resort. In this case the local record office only has a photocopy of the tithe award while the original is in the National Library of Wales, which holds all the diocesan copies of Welsh awards.

Example: Yateley, Hampshire

The extent to which a tithe map and schedule can add to the understanding of a community and its development can be illustrated through a case study of the old Hampshire village of Yateley, some 35 miles south-west of the centre of London, which even in the 19th century attracted some commuters. Originally an area of subsistence farming, by the time of the tithe award the agricultural community included a number of better off farmers with some absentee landlords (who themselves were in several instances the descendants of 18th-century inhabitants of the village).

The tithe map and apportionment schedule make it possible to reconstruct land use in a vivid way.

The actual apportionment is dated 22nd September 1846 but the map (fig.27) and schedule itself (fig.28) are earlier (no later than 1844, with the award of rent charge being dated 13th March 1844). There is a still earlier schedule. The base survey and map appear to have been created for the parish as early as 1839. The map – which actually points in the direction of magnetic north! – was signed off by George Hewitt, land surveyor and valuer of Elvetham (Hants) and Oxford. Although not, it seems, a designated first class map, it is actually quite accurate and was used subsequently in connection with land transfers and other legal business. In carrying out his valuations of meadow land, Hewitt was constrained by an early 17th-century court case which valued meadow land at 2d (less than 1p) an acre – an unrealistic valuation even in 1604.

The tithe map and apportionment schedule make it possible to reconstruct land use in a vivid way. Using these maps and the schedule alongside local records and walks around the village, a detailed picture of the community emerges, although, as with other places, the tithing does not cover the whole parish. The modern land use map (fig.29) puts into sharp relief the

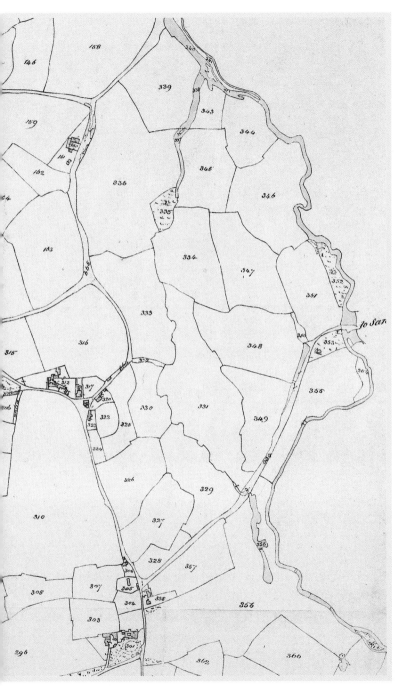

FIGURE 27: *Yateley Tithe Map, 1844, showing the village centre. There is another version of the map (not simply a copy) at The National Archives.* (Hampshire Record Office)

FIGURE 28: *An extract from the Yateley Tithe Apportionment, 1844.* (Hampshire Record Office)

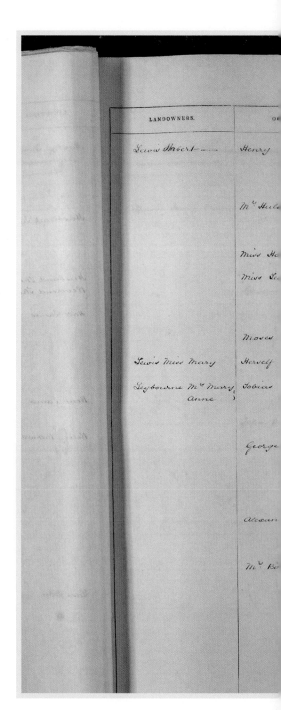

scattered nature of the village which is largely formed of a collection of hamlets, each clustered round a 'green' – at Yateley proper, Cricket Hill, Darby Green and at Frogmore – with a few larger farmsteads scattered evenly across the village. These greens were common land, and gave easy access onto larger areas of the common beyond. Each green can clearly be seen with houses around it.

The extract from the large tithe map shows clearly Yateley green, the centre of the village, with its buildings and cottages. Prominent buildings include the part-Saxon church (plot 200), the Vicarage (plot 169 and now known as Glebe House), the Old Dog and Partridge pub (plot 189) and Hall Place (plots 205/206 and now known as Yateley Manor). Roughly half the houses and cottages in this area – which date from the 14th to the 19th centuries – are still in existence.

Although some houses were being 'gentrified', many of the cottages

10.

C.C.—London: Printed and Published (By Authority,) by Shaw and Sons, Fetter-lane.

Numbers referring to the Plan.	NAME AND DESCRIPTION OF LANDS AND PREMISES.	STATE OF CULTIVATION.	QUANTITIES IN STATUTE MEASURE.			Amount of Rent-Charge apportioned upon the several Lands, and Payable to the Appropriator			REMARKS.
			A.	R.	P.	£	s.	d.	
171	House and Garden	————	"	3	30	"	6	6	
172	Kirk ————	Grass ————	3	3	26	"	"	8	
173	ditto ————	" ————	4	1	3	"	"	7	
			9	"	19	"	7	10	
173a	Driftway ————	————	"	"	13	"	"	"	
174	House and Garden	————	"	1	34	"	3	"	
			"	2	7	"	3	"	
175	House and Garden	————	"	1	16	"	2	6	
176	Pightle ————	Grass ————	"	3	12	"	"	2	
176a	Driftway ————	————	"	"	4	"	"	"	
180	Pasture ————	Grass ————	"	2	5	"	"	1	
			1	1	21	"	"	3	
178	House and Garden	————	"	"	15				
177	House and Garden	————	"	1	13	"	2	5	
349	Weighbridge Meadow	Grass ————	4	2	13	"	"	9	
354	ditto ————	" ————	"	1	14	"	"	1	
355	ditto ————	" ————	5	"	19	"	"	10	
			10	"	6	"	1	8	
384	Little Meadow ————	Grass ————	"	2	10	"	"	1	
502	House and Garden	————	"	1	7	"	2	"	
508	Pightle ————	Grass ————	"	3	12	"	"	2	
540	Layberds ————	Arable ————	1	1	4	"	3	10	
			2	3	33	"	6	1	
440	Garden ————	————	"	1	27	"	2	"	
441	House and Garden	————	1	2	29	"	9	6	
			2	"	16	"	11	6	
516	House and Garden	————	"	1	3	"	2	"	
517	Millgrove Field ————	Arable ————	9	1	30	1	3	9	
518	Millgrove Little Meadow	Grass ————	4	3	22	"	"	10	
519	" Great Meadow	" ————	8	1	28	"	1	5	
523	The Slip ————	" ————	"	3	7	"	"	2	
			23	3	10	1	8	2	

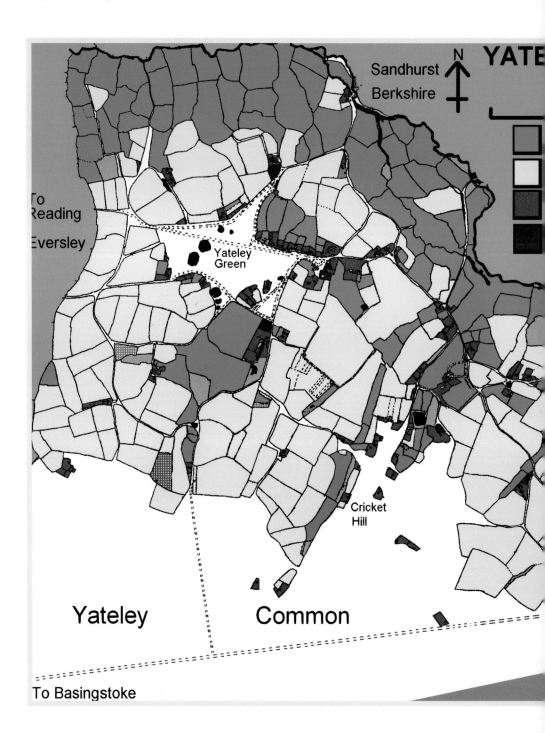

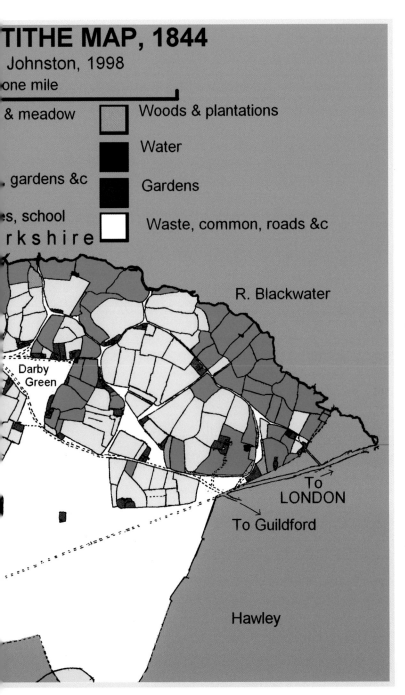

TITHE MAP, 1844

Johnston, 1998

one mile

& meadow — Woods & plantations

Water

gardens &c — Gardens

s, school — Waste, common, roads &c

r k s h i r e

R. Blackwater

Darby
Green

To
LONDON

To Guildford

Hawley

FIGURE 29: *Yateley Tithing Land Use Map – modern reconstruction. A court case of 1604 fixed meadow land at just under 1p an acre!* (Courtesy Richard Johnston)

concentrated around the greens – or commons – were occupied by less well-off families with holdings of about four acres and rights to use the commons. Since animals were not allowed to be kept on the commons overnight, the one or two fields next to a cottage were of considerable importance. Whilst these cottagers were clearly in a better position than the true poor who had no land, they would have had to eke out a living by making cloth or shoes. As factory methods spread, such supplemental sources of income would have come under increasing pressure.

The apportionment, in particular, helps to reveal a land-holding pattern where at least the better off farmers had land near the river for early hay, as well as arable land on higher ground. Field sizes, not perhaps surprisingly, reflected their use, with the meadows nearer the river generally being larger than the arable fields. The records also reveal that the land deteriorated in quality as one got nearer to the upland common (the white areas on the lower part of the land use map), which in turn helps to explain the choice of crops (malting grain and hops). These crops, in any case, enjoyed a ready market in the form of an expanding beer industry. Despite the presence of richer farmers, the largest of the agricultural holdings, Hall Place, still represented only a small percentage of the total land area in the village – a fact which reinforced the character of the village as an 'open' one where no landlord could exert unbridled influence. The tithe records, with their evidence on landholding, land occupiers and land use, clearly help (combined with other evidence) to create a picture of Yateley as a modest, but socially and economically differentiated, community made up of (often absentee) landlords, professional people, yeoman tenant farmers and poorer inhabitants (with and without land).

Three copies of an award were originally produced: one for the parish, one for the diocese and one for the Commissioners.

■ Locating the maps

Three copies of an award were originally produced: one for the parish, one for the diocese and one for the Commissioners. The parish and diocesan copies for English parishes are increasingly likely to be found at the county record office, with the Commissioners' copy at The National Archives. Papers relating to tithes may also be located still in parish, estate and solicitors' holdings. Record offices like Cheshire have digitised

LIMITATIONS OF TITHE MAPS & SCHEDULES

Tithe maps and schedules, of course, have their limitations as a source. Not all areas were subject to an award and even within a tithe district where tithable areas exist, non-tithable areas can be effectively ignored. A parish might contain more than one tithing which means that an award gives only a partial picture of a community. Neighbouring farms can, unfortunately, even be in separate tithings. Although tithes were not simply a rural problem, many urban and industrial areas were not subject to them and therefore are not mapped. Many tithe maps, too, are based on out of date or inferior maps, which can add to the normal problems of interpretation. Nevertheless, for the family historian they can be fruitfully compared with the somewhat later large-scale OS maps.

their collections, making access to them easier.

Finding a tithe survey has become much easier thanks to the indispensable work of Kain and Oliver (see below). To access the records held at The National Archives it becomes a simple matter of adding a TNA reference as a prefix to the reference found in this source. There is also valuable advice in the book written for The National Archives by Beech and Mitchell. If the parish is known there is need only to type into the computerized (and online) catalogue the parish name and the IR (Inland Revenue) Series number. Maps, which are often the best place to start, are in IR 30 with apportionments (and altered apportionments) in IR 29. The tithe files are to be found in IR 18.

R.J.P. Kain and R.R. Oliver, *The Tithe Maps of England and Wales* (Cambridge, 1995).

G. Beech and R. Mitchell, *Maps for Family and Local History: The Records of the Tithe, Valuation Office and National Farm Surveys of England and Wales 1836-1943* (2nd ed., TNA, 2004).

Robert Davies, *The Tithe Maps of Wales* (Aberystwyth, 1999).

———————●●►———————

Valuation Office Survey 1910-15

ALTHOUGH THE TITHE AWARDS ARE A RICH AND INCOMPARABLE SOURCE OF INFORMATION ON LAND OWNERSHIP AND OCCUPANCY IN THE 1840S, FAMILY HISTORIANS INTERESTED IN TRACING EDWARDIAN ANCESTORS HAVE AN EVEN MORE COMPREHENSIVE SURVEY THEY CAN CONSULT – THE VALUATION OFFICE SURVEY, OR 'SECOND DOMESDAY' AS IT IS SOMETIMES KNOWN. ALTHOUGH THESE RECORDS ARE BECOMING BETTER KNOWN, THEY REMAIN UNDER-UTILISED BY BOTH FAMILY AND LOCAL HISTORIANS.

The maps and books of reference are a mine of information on the owners and occupiers of virtually all rural and urban property c.1912 and the properties in which they lived. They include information on the construction, extent and use of a property, what water and sanitary facilities there are, the rent payable and the property's valuation. The date of building may be recorded and with earlier surveys of rural property there may be a sketched plan of the farm or house. Although the level of detail recorded varies from valuer to valuer, there are descriptions of every kind of property in the community (including cinemas, which were just making their appearance) and the use to which the land was put. The information on farms, industrial premises and, sometimes, domestic premises can be sufficiently detailed that their layout can be reconstructed. Used in conjunction with the census, local directories, rate books and local health records, it is possible to identify who was resident in which house, what the house was like as a place to live, who the neighbours were and what employment, shopping and other facilities existed locally. Working class communities swept away by later slum clearance programmes can be recreated.

The Survey, launched as a result of the Finance Act of 1910, was the intended prelude to the introduction of new taxes, notably a self-explanatory Increment Value Duty, and involved a comprehensive valuation of rural and urban property which was largely completed before the end of 1915. (Scotland was surveyed in a similar manner in 1911-12, whilst Ireland, which had been subject to annual property valuations since the time of the so-called 'Griffith's Valuation' of 1848-64, was less fully covered.)

The boundary of each unit of private property (or 'hereditament') was carefully marked on a larger-scale OS map, usually using red or pink (although other colours and colour wash were also used). Only private land was coloured in this way. The valuers used 25-inch, large-scale OS maps – or maps of a greater scale for urban locations. Some updating of these maps was carried out, making them a useful source for family historians in their own right. A recent edition was used whenever possible, although some of the base maps dated back to the 1880s or earlier. Whilst carrying out the valuations in the field, working maps were used which, if they still exist, are usually in local record offices. Often incomplete, they nevertheless can be useful and may have penciled annotations. The maps must be used with the relevant written records.

Whilst carrying out the valuations in the field, working maps were used which, if they still exist, are usually in local record offices.

VALUATION AND FIELD BOOKS

Local valuers used Valuation Books (containing basic information derived from tax and rate sources and a return from landlords) when they undertook inspections and recorded their findings in Field Books. The unique hereditament (property) number which was initially recorded in the Valuation Book was added to the plot on the map in red or black. Where a hereditament consisted of several parts, a suffix was added. This number allowed cross-linking to entries in the Field Books which were organised according to Income Tax Parishes (ITPs), themselves subsumed under Valuation Districts. These ITPs could cover a single (large) parish or, more likely, a number of parishes and were labelled according to the first parish in each book. Only in a few cases were street indexes made. The ITPs are marked on the maps, frequently in yellow.

Although much more comprehensive than the earlier tithe records, not every property was included and matters of no direct concern – what land was being used for, for instance – do not receive systematic attention. Land owned by public utility companies, like railways, was often missed due to a shortage of time and there were also certain other, more official, omissions. Even when the four-page Field Book entry for a property is found, the degree of detail can vary enormously.

Since the task was to value each property, one can expect to find the address, the owner's and occupier's names, the extent of the property, the owner's interest (freehold, copyhold or leasehold), the rent (and whether paid weekly, monthly, or yearly), who was responsible for rates, repairs and insurance (owner, tenant or both), and various calculations worked out by the valuer. Many of the basic details were copied in from the Valuation Books as a precursor to the inspections.

As a short cut there was a strong tendency to give detail about one property and then refer back similar properties to the earlier 'model' one.

As a short cut there was a strong tendency to give detail about one property and then refer back similar properties to the earlier 'model' one. With rows of terraced houses, therefore, you should expect to have to consult the 'model' record as well as the specific property you are interested in. The danger in such an approach is that it misses idiosyncrasies of individual properties, since terraces that look as if they may have been constructed together were often composites of groups of housing built at different times (as can often been seen by studying roof lines and joins). Different valuers in any case filled in the Field Book entries with varying degrees of thoroughness, according to their own style of working and time constraints. Depending on the surveyor, one can find an indication of the construction and condition of the property, room dimensions, whether a three-roomed cottage was a 'one up and two down' or the other way around, the rent (although the rent could be aggregated for a number of properties rather than be shown individually) and whether a household shared water taps, WCs and the back yard. Although multiple occupation of a property may be indicated, there are no details of these occupiers given.

Some of this information can be checked against local Medical Officer of Heath and other sanitary records – as many MOHs, at this time, were under pressure to act on housing legislation and enforce local bye-laws. For rural holdings one can often find a sketch plan (until 1912) and some information on land use and the state of cultivation. Sometimes, the Field Books continued to have entries added years after the Survey finished, which can be useful.

Perhaps the crucial point to make is that by using the maps and Field Books, addresses given in the censuses can be positively linked to a location. This is also very helpful when using directories (which do record house numbers, for some properties at least, with a degree of accuracy) and rate books (that don't generally do so). Where properties are subdivided into discrete dwellings, it can be difficult, in the absence of such sources, to identify which property is which and which household is living where. For some streets, house numbering can be checked against the Goad maps (see Chapter 5), although care must be taken to check the actual date of revision being shown for a particular area of a Goad map. The census gives no details on the owners of property or the use of rooms and offers less information on the number of rooms a property has. On the other hand, the Field Books are concerned with owners and the main occupiers(s), not families as a whole.

Sometimes the Field Books continued to have entries added years after the Survey finished, which can be useful.

Example: Dundas Street, York

What can be achieved using the Valuation Survey, in conjunction with other contemporary records, can be illustrated by a case study of a slum street in York called Dundas Street. Apart from the relevant Valuation Office maps and Field Books, consulted at The National Archives, a number of other, locally available, sources were used. These included the census (in this case the 1901; using the 1911 Census will of course give even greater immediacy to the results), local newspapers (with indexes), Kelly's Directory for 1905, Cooke's Directory for 1909, a rate book of 1914 for the area concerned and local health records (which included the investigations and findings of the local MOH and sanitary inspectors).

Using such records it is possible to work out exactly where the households listed in the census lived in the street, roughly how long they lived there, who the neighbours and local shopkeepers were, what businesses operated in the street, what

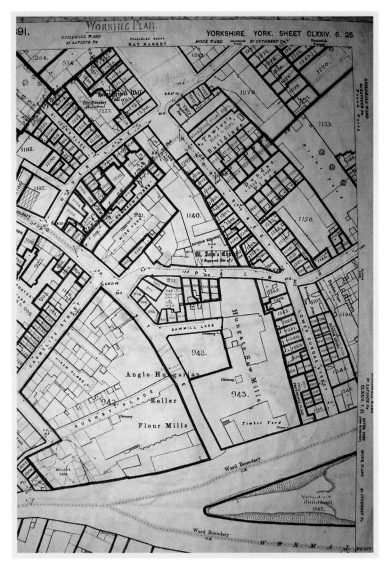

FIGURE 30: *Valuation Office map sheet, York. Houses are clearly distinguished by hereditament numbers although these are not logically arranged.* (The National Archives)

the main local sources of employment would have been, what the housing conditions were like and, even, whether or not a household had to pop across the road to use the toilet (which was, sometimes, literally the case).

Dundas Street was one of the three principal streets in a slum district of York known as Hungate. The map (fig.30) shows clearly the houses (with their hereditament numbers) and the location. The area was subject to a slum clearance scheme in the 1930s, although it was still possible to walk down parts of its cobbled street until the latest spate of residential and commercial development in 2008. What the houses commented on by the valuer looked like can be seen from old photographs of the street that were taken prior to the slum clearance (fig.31). As can be traced in the Field Books (fig.32), the street consisted of mostly two-, three- or four-roomed properties that were built of brick with pantiled roofs and whose inhabitants often shared water taps and sanitary facilities.

Among the local businesses were two established provision shopkeepers, boot and shoe makers working from home and a slaughter house! Rent levels fluctuated according to location and size of property, but nearly all the rents given were what may be labelled 'slum rents'. A family living in Lower Dundas Street – or one of the poor courts leading off the street – could expect to pay lower rents to their landlords, sometimes as little as 2 shillings (10 pence) a week.

FIGURE 3I: *Part of Dundas Street, York. In the 1930s all these properties were demolished and the inhabitants relocated to a new housing estate.* (York City Archives)

Although the details that are given are often brief they are still informative. No.13 Lower Dundas Street (hereditament no.1259) is described as a 'Three roomed cottage. Two down one up. Small yard, earth closet, water in house. Roofs [sic] pantiled.' No.12a Dundas Street (hereditament no.1204) had an extent of 34 yards and was owned by Leetham's Flour Mill. Leetham's mill dominated the skyline and seems to have provided some of the labourers in the street with their means

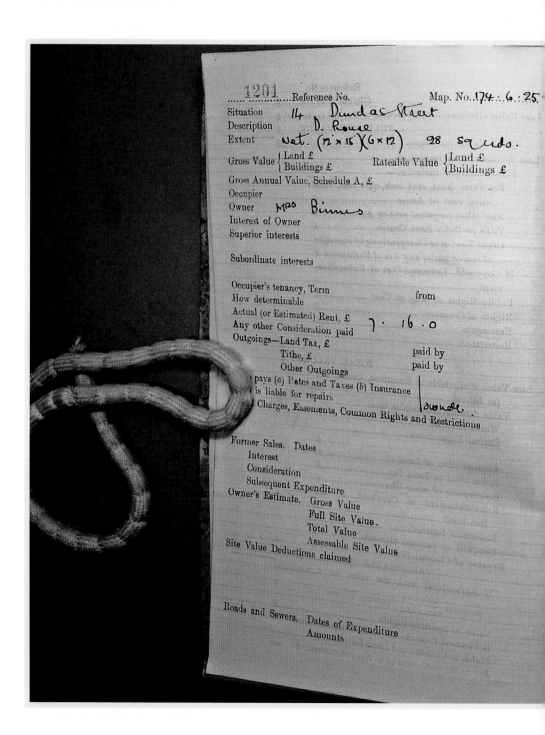

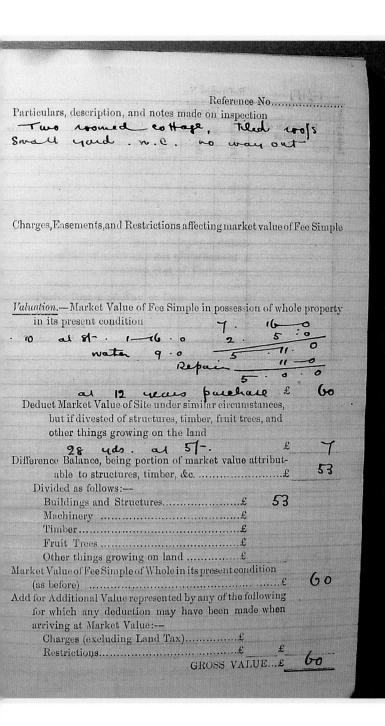

Reference No.......................

Particulars, description, and notes made on inspection

Two roomed cottage. Tiled roofs. Small yard. w.c. no way out

Charges,Easements,and Restrictions affecting market value of Fee Simple

Valuation.—Market Value of Fee Simple in possession of whole property in its present condition

10 at 8/- . 1—16 . 0
water 9 . 0
Repair

7 . 16 . 0
2 . 5 . 0
5 . 11 . 0
11 . 0
5 . 0 . 0

at 12 years purchase £ 60

Deduct Market Value of Site under similar circumstances, but if divested of structures, timber, fruit trees, and other things growing on the land

28 yds . at 5/- . £ *7*

Difference Balance, being portion of market value attributable to structures, timber, &c. ....£ *53*

Divided as follows:—

Buildings and Structures.....................£ *53*
Machinery ....£
Timber..£
Fruit Trees ....£
Other things growing on land ....£

Market Value of Fee Simple of Whole in its present condition (as before) ....£ *60*

Add for Additional Value represented by any of the following for which any deduction may have been made when arriving at Market Value:—

Charges (excluding Land Tax)..............£
Restrictions.......................................£   £
GROSS VALUE...£ *60*

FIGURE 32: *Valuation Office Field Book house entry. Entries consist of two double pages but the first double page, as shown, is the more informative for family historians. (The National Archives)*

of employment. Wages were notoriously low and the mill showered the area with dust to the detriment of the, already poor, health of its poverty-stricken neighbours. The inhabitants of this particular house had to share both water tap and wc with two other households.

Cross-checking the records reveals an interesting situation regarding Nos. 4 and 5 Higher, or Upper, Dundas Street. According to the Valuation Office Survey, No. 5, consisting of a kitchen and two bedrooms, was occupied by Thomas Haw, whilst at No. 4 lived Henry March. Both these men were labourers and long-term residents of the street, with March employed at Leetham's mills according to the 1901 Census. As recorded in this same census, however, Haw is living at No. 4 and March at No.5, a fact confirmed by the MOH's own careful inspection of the area in 1907. Either the occupiers' names were transposed at some point during the valuation process (and not necessarily by the valuer himself) – which is perfectly possible – or the two families switched houses, something which was quite easy to do since the properties were only being rented. The 1914 rate book places Haw at No.5 (thereby agreeing with the Valuation Office Survey) but puts March at No. 3!

Fortunately, Cooke's 1909 directory – which precedes the survey and is more thorough than many directories – appears to confirm that the change recorded by the valuer was due to a house move (probably in 1908) and not human error. The reason could be that No.4 was 6d a week cheaper to rent. March had once been a fitter and may have been downwardly mobile at this point in time. Even in a poor street, socio-economic status could be based on which house and which part of the street one lived in. Higher Dundas Street was, on the whole, a better place to live in than Lower Dundas Street, which was subject to flooding from the less than salubrious River Foss and was seen by residents themselves as of lower status.

Valuers were conscious of any factor that could affect values.

Valuers were conscious of any factor that could affect values. Recording the use and dimensions of buildings could be seen as part of the assessment process, although many settled for total floor space in the case of a less significant property. Often enough detail is given on domestic and commercial or industrial properties to have a good idea of their layout. Anything that affected values, including rights of way, could potentially be added to a Field Book entry. Significant changes to property had to be recorded when known. In 1914 the valuer added to the Field Book of 2 Lower Dundas Street (hereditament no. 1234) that this, and some of the other cottages in that part of the street, had now been converted into 'double houses'.

Much, too, can be learned about the owners of local businesses who were often core members of their communities. Unlike many of their customers, who would either seek to move to better housing or, because they were aged or infirm, might be forced into the workhouse, they often resided in the same property or street for long periods. No.14 High Dundas Street was owned (though not occupied) by Annie Binns, who also owned the provision shop next door. The Binns family had run the shop at No.15 since at least the start of the century and were well-known in the area. Running a shop in an area where tenants could only afford to buy in small quantities and relied on the credit provided by the shopkeeper was clearly a sensible thing to do.

Much, too, can be learned about the owners of local businesses who were often core members of their communities.

Whilst Annie and her shop can be easily traced in the directories and the 1914 rate book (where she is listed as its owner), we rely on the Valuation records to identify most of the owners. The 1914 rate book lists few owners and directories like Kelly's (though not Cooke's) are only interested in some of the more significant local residents. Another local business run by the same person (in this case William Empson) for a considerable period of time was the Bricklayer's Arms, strategically situated between the two halves of the street and on the corner of Palmer Lane (hereditament No. 1265). The Field Book identifies this property as six-roomed and owner-occupied, but pertinently adds that it is a 'poor property & locality'. Unlike shops such as those of Annie Binns, pubs were under pressure from temperance reformers and working men's clubs in this period. A number of York pubs had already been closed down by the local authority as surplus to requirements.

The Valuation records, as one can see, allow us to link together the various sources with a reassuring degree of certainty and completeness. The map allows the family historian to picture the community in which their ancestor lived.

■ Locating the maps

The Valuation records can be quite hard to identify at The National Archives because the Field Books (Series IR 58) – of which some 95,000 volumes survive – are unfortunately stored within valuation districts by Income Tax Parish. Local record offices should have the Valuation Books (where they survive) but these will be stored under more recent valuation districts rather than those operational at the time of the Survey. Locally, one should also check for any so-called 'working map' which the valuer used whilst he worked.

The final maps and Field Books are only to be found at The National Archives. The maps are stored at IR 121 and IR 124-145 according to Valuation Office region and then Valuation District. The Yorkshire region for instance (containing York of course) is IR 134. York is a Valuation District (no 10) so the reference becomes IR134/10. The final part of the reference – 979 – denotes the actual map needed. The on-line catalogue of The National Archives can be used to find the full reference (http://www.nationalarchives.gov.uk/catalogue).

The maps are a good starting point for identifying the required hereditament number which is needed to access the Field Books, although the Valuation Books are equally good for this purpose. A Valuation Book for an Income Tax Parish will indicate the parishes that are included and, for urban areas, there may be a street index as well. Some local societies are now showing an interest in such records and occasionally, as with the Two Villages Trust for Milton Keynes village (www.mkheritage.co.uk/tva/index.html) and the Northumberland Communities website (http://communities.northumberland.gov.uk), some information has been made available online.

G. Beech and R. Mitchell, *Maps for Family and Local History: The Records of the Tithe, Valuation Office and National Farm Surveys of England and Wales 1836-1943* (2nd ed., TNA, 2004).

Brian Short and Mick Reed, *Landownership and Society in Edwardian England and Wales: The Finance (1909-10) Act 1910 Records* (University of Sussex, 1987).

8

National Farm Survey 1941-43

THE NATIONAL FARM SURVEY PROVIDES A VALUABLE SNAPSHOT OF FARMING COMMUNITIES AT A PARTICULAR POINT IN TIME AND COVERS A GREAT MANY MORE FARMS THAN THE EARLIER TITHE SURVEYS. SINCE THE RECORDS FALL WITHIN LIVING MEMORY IT IS ALSO POSSIBLE TO ASSESS THE RECORDS IN THE LIGHT OF ORAL TESTIMONY FROM WITHIN THE FAMILY. AS WITH ALL RECORDS THEY WERE PRODUCED FOR A SPECIFIC PURPOSE WHICH ACCOUNTS FOR THEIR PARTICULAR EMPHASIS AND WHICH NEEDS TO BE APPRECIATED. IN THIS CASE – MIDWAY THROUGH THE SECOND WORLD WAR AND WITH A POPULATION FACING SERIOUS FOOD SHORTAGES – THERE WAS CONCERN ABOUT THE STATE OF FARMS AND THEIR MANAGEMENT AT A TIME WHEN THE GOVERNMENT WAS TRYING TO MAXIMIZE YIELDS AND BRING AS MUCH LAND AS POSSIBLE INTO CULTIVATION.

The records, therefore, show interest in the farmer and how he was running the farm; the crops grown and the acreage; the livestock and the flocks that he kept; the facilities available on the farm (water and electricity, for example); and the man/horse/mechanical power in use. Although one can expect to know the numbers and ages of those working on the farm (as relatives or workers) the records, on the whole, are not interested in identifying particular individuals – beyond the owners and occupiers of the 300,000 or so farms, of five acres or more, to be found across England and Wales. This does not, however, mean that it is never possible to discover the identity of other members of the family or those working on the farm.

As these are parish-based records, consisting of maps and accompanying forms, the family historian can locate all relations having farms in the parish and identify neighbouring farms and farmers as well. There is a wealth of detail about types and methods of farming and, where the farm or smallholding was not a full-time job for the farmer concerned, what else he did to earn a living. Although very small farms were excluded from the survey and farmers did sometimes resist taking part in the survey, information is included on market gardeners and farmers with smallholdings. It is likely, therefore, that an ancestor owning or occupying a farm at this time will figure in the Survey.

The records for each farm are made up of an OS map, a so-called Primary Farm Record and three census forms. All the forms are printed and arranged to elicit standard answers, often of a numerical or yes/no kind, wherever possible and appropriate. As with earlier surveys, the map and textual records need to be used together. The map shows the farm and its boundaries (delineated by a coloured pencil, crayon or ink boundary or full shading) and adds the reference number. Where a farm is made up of a number of parcels of land, the same reference number is given to each. The maps can also record extraneous information like playing fields and even golf courses. Unfortunately, although the situation varies from county to county, perhaps 10 % of the maps are thought to be missing from the records.

It is likely that an ancestor owning or occupying a farm at this time will figure in the Survey.

The Primary Farm Record (the inspector's report on his visit to the farm) and the main agricultural census return for 4th June 1941 are the two principal written texts but are accompanied, in most cases, by two supplemental census forms. The first of these, essentially to do with market gardening, is often of little relevance unless the farmer concerned was a market gardener or heavily involved in producing fruit and other crops of this kind. In many cases the form is blank, except perhaps for the section on hay and straw. The other supplemental form is of more interest, addressing as it does tenure; the rent payable; labour (differentiating between family and non-family farm workers, as well as between part-time workers who worked part of each week and those who worked part of each year); and motive power (the use of tractors, stationary engines and horses). Because this form expanded on some questions already included in the main census form and asked personal questions that farmers did not necessarily want to answer, a percentage of the farmers simply ignored the form (and failed to return it).

MAIN AGRICULTURAL CENSUS FORM

The most useful of the three forms was the main agricultural census form, which farmers were familiar with because they had to fill one in every year anyway. In a sense, the whole survey can be seen as a greatly expanded quantitative (and qualitative) census with this form at its heart. This principal census form is mainly concerned with crop acreages, the amount of pasture and rough grazing and the numbers of animals, and, despite the way it structures responses using boxes, is informative. How land was used – whether a farm was arable or mixed – is of interest to any family historian trying to find out about life on the farm (and was of particular interest to the Government in 1941). Already, by the time of this census, there had been a drive to plough up land for crops, some of which had not been cultivated for centuries.

The most interesting of the forms, however, is the Primary Farm Record. Not only is the name and address of the occupier given (and, if different, the name and address of the owner), but the inspector, who was usually a local farmer himself, had to make qualitative assessments of the farm and the farmer. Based on an actual visit to the farm wherever possible, the general remarks section of the form can be very detailed and offers much information on the condition of the farm and suggests improvements to farming methods. Unfortunately, in many parishes, the inspector concerned recorded no remarks at all.

The inspector was also asked, controversially, to grade the ability of the farmer according to one of three categories – A, B, or C. If a grade C was indicated the inspector was supposed to explain what 'personal failings' accounted for this decision. The great majority of farmers were classed as A or B – which required no explanation – and in the case of the minority classed as grade C there was a reluctance to comment on the character of the farmer. Although they could be described as lazy or indifferent, the inspector preferred to refer to the poor quality of the land or the shortage of manpower and other factors beyond the farmer's personal control – such as the farmer having being widowed or, even, gassed during the First World War. One reason, no doubt, was the fact that the inspector was himself likely to be a local man.

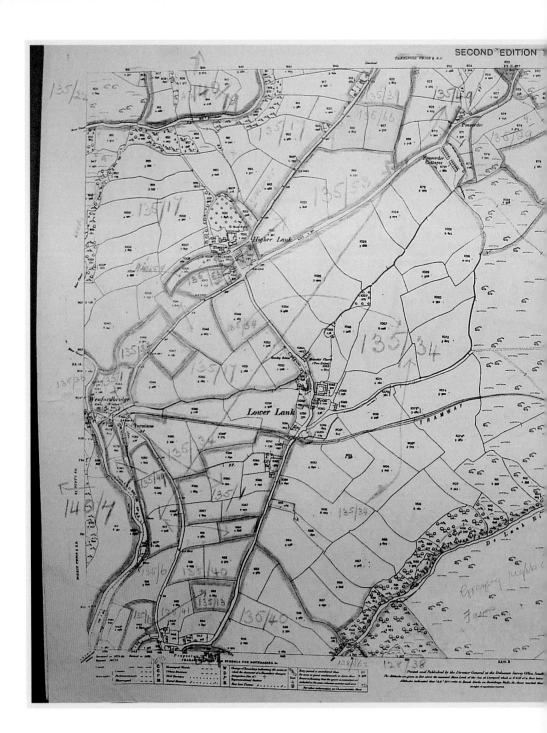

FIGURE 33: *Map showing De Lank Farm.* (The National Archives)

Example: De Lank Farm, St Breward

To fully appreciate the nature of the information contained in the records, one needs to look at a particular set. The farm chosen is De Lank Farm situated in St Breward parish, some ten miles from Bodmin in Cornwall. This farm, with its 16th-century farmhouse, had been bought by Charles Masters senior (born 1876) in 1911 at an estate sale. (Also traceable in the National Farm Survey records, is the farm of another relation, John Masters of Bradford, Blisland (No. 135/73); both Charles Masters and John Masters, incidentally, are listed under 'Commercial' in the 1926 Kelly Directory.)

Also referenced in the survey of De Lank is the small holding at Pendrift which the family continued to farm even after it was decided to purchase De Lank in 1911 to accommodate the needs of a growing household of four sons. The main census form correctly records the fact that the farm had been in the family's ownership for 29 years.

To fully appreciate the nature of the information contained in the National Farm Survey records, one needs to look at a particular set.

The farm is clearly shown on the map as 135/34 (fig.33). The map is the 1907 Second Edition 25 inch (reduced) OS map of the area. (Frequently, 6-inch maps were used in the Survey but these can become quite crowded.) As usual, colour is used to distinguish the farm's boundaries which oral testimony confirms are accurate. The lane from Higher Lank to Penvorder served as the farm's northern border with acreage stretching down to the De Lank River. To the west, part of the farm bordered on Wenford, whilst to the east the farm took in the area around De Lank quarries. (A tramway used to cross the farm taking stone from the quarries to the railway connection at Wenford.) Visible on the map, too, is the farmhouse itself and its quadrangle of (covered) farm buildings. These buildings are now converted to tourist lets.

Interestingly, the typed name of Charles Masters (senior), as owner, is crossed through on an envelope stamped 23rd June 1941 and the names of CA and WR Masters added by hand in its stead. These sets of initials are those of two of his sons, Charles Alexander and Walter Rogers Masters. At the time, Charles Masters senior was about to marry for the second time and charge of the farm was being handed over to these two sons. Both men had been actively working on the farm since childhood. Walter Masters (1911-1967; fig.34) often in later life recalled the 1930s when, in order to put food on the table during the Depression, he was obliged to sell turnips produced on the farm around the village. Walter is shown as the farm's occupier because his brother Charles Alexander and family lived in a cottage across the road.

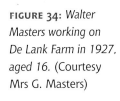

FIGURE 34: *Walter Masters working on De Lank Farm in 1927, aged 16.* (Courtesy Mrs G. Masters)

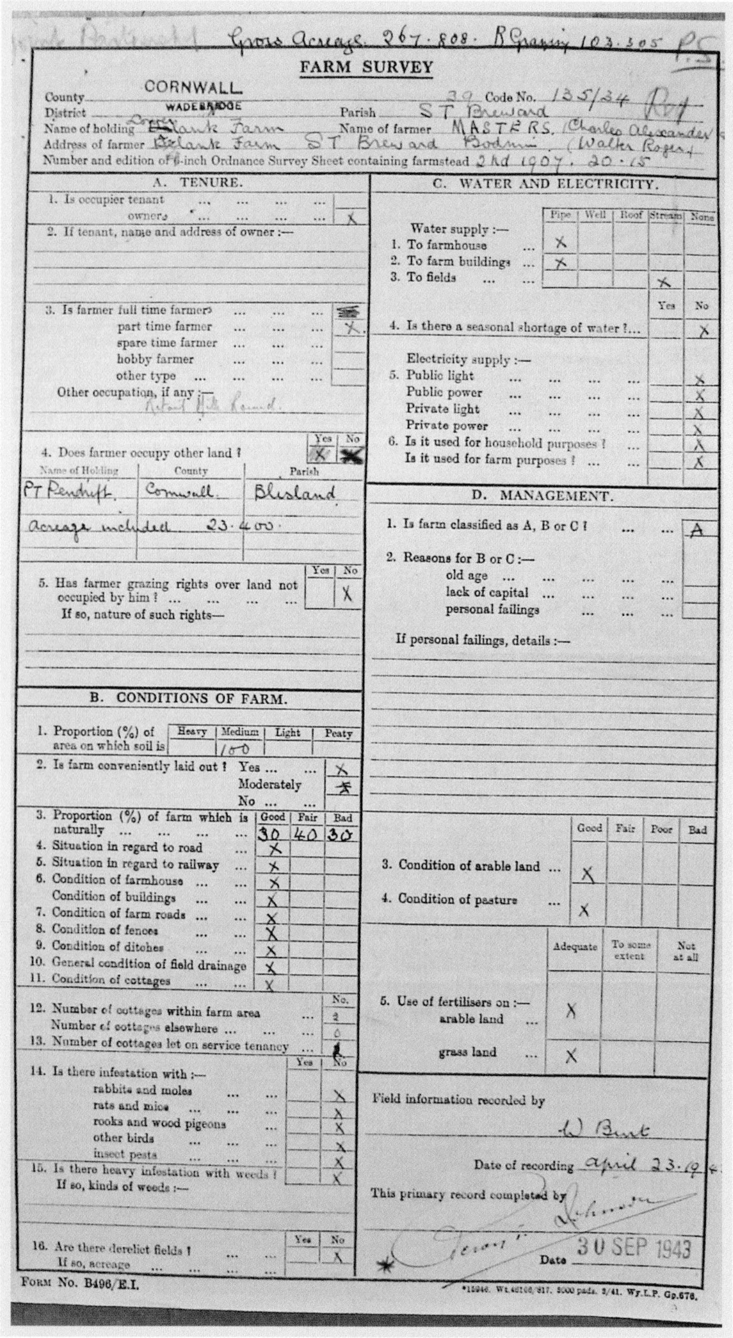

Gross Acreage 267·808 R Grazing 103·305

FARM SURVEY

County CORNWALL

District WADEBRIDGE

39 Code No. 135/34

Parish ST Breward

Name of holding De Lank Farm

Name of farmer MASTERS, Charles Alexander

Address of farmer De Lank Farm ST Breward Bodmin (Walter Rogers)

Number and edition of 6-inch Ordnance Survey Sheet containing farmstead 2nd 1907. 20·15

A. TENURE.

1. Is occupier tenant
owner ... X
2. If tenant, name and address of owner :—
3. Is farmer full time farmer
part time farmer ... X
spare time farmer
hobby farmer
other type
Other occupation, if any :—

4. Does farmer occupy other land ? Yes X

Name of Holding	County	Parish
PT Pendrift	Cornwall	Blisland
acreage included	23·400	

5. Has farmer grazing rights over land not occupied by him ? No X
If so, nature of such rights—

B. CONDITIONS OF FARM.

1. Proportion (%) of area on which soil is

Heavy	Medium	Light	Peaty
	100		

2. Is farm conveniently laid out ? Yes ... X
Moderately
No ...

	Good	Fair	Bad
3. Proportion (%) of farm which is naturally	30	40	30
4. Situation in regard to road	X		
5. Situation in regard to railway	X		
6. Condition of farmhouse	X		
Condition of buildings	X		
7. Condition of farm roads	X		
8. Condition of fences	X		
9. Condition of ditches	X		
10. General condition of field drainage	X		
11. Condition of cottages	X		

	No.
12. Number of cottages within farm area	2
Number of cottages elsewhere	0
13. Number of cottages let on service tenancy	1

14. Is there infestation with :—	Yes	No
rabbits and moles		X
rats and mice		X
rooks and wood pigeons		X
other birds		X
insect pests		X
15. Is there heavy infestation with weeds ?		X

If so, kinds of weeds :—

	Yes	No
16. Are there derelict fields ? If so, acreage		X

C. WATER AND ELECTRICITY.

Water supply :—	Pipe	Well	Roof	Stream	None
1. To farmhouse	X				
2. To farm buildings	X				
3. To fields				X	

	Yes	No
4. Is there a seasonal shortage of water ?		X
Electricity supply :—		
5. Public light		X
Public power		X
Private light		X
Private power		X
6. Is it used for household purposes ?		X
Is it used for farm purposes ?		X

D. MANAGEMENT.

1. Is farm classified as A, B or C ? ... A
2. Reasons for B or C :—
old age
lack of capital
personal failings
If personal failings, details :—

	Good	Fair	Poor	Bad
3. Condition of arable land	X			
4. Condition of pasture	X			

5. Use of fertilisers on :—	Adequate	To some extent	Not at all
arable land	X		
grass land	X		

Field information recorded by W Burt

Date of recording April 23.1941

This primary record completed by

Date 30 SEP 1943

Form No. B496/E.I.

*15946. Wt.46166/817. 5000 pads. 3/41. Wy.L.P. Gp.676.

FIGURE 35: *National Farm Survey Primary Record for De Lank Farm – front.* (The National Archives)

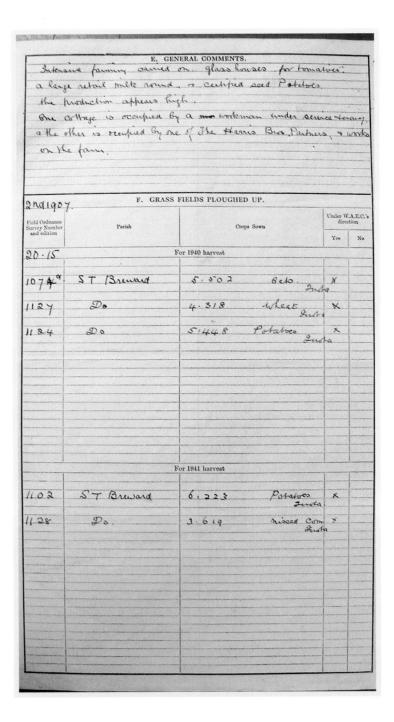

FIGURE 36: *National Farm Survey Primary Record for De Lank Farm – back.* (The National Archives)

The Primary Record (figs.35 and 36) gives a category 'A' rating to the farmers of this farm. This rating was by far the most common. The Masters brothers, however, potentially risked a lower rating because of their involvement with a milk round (run principally by Charles Alexander). Inspectors – or at least the government committees in charge of the Survey – often didn't like farmers being distracted from their main farming role by having part-time work. The milk round, however, was clearly an offshoot of the farm's normal activities and this was probably taken into account. No doubt unknown to the inspector was the fact that the retail milk round – operated from a car, not a van (fig.37) – in fact helped to pay the farm workers' wages!

As was usually true of the Survey forms, the total crop acreage is written on the top of the form by hand (there was nowhere on the form to record it); together, in this case, with the amount of rough grazing. The general remarks of the inspector indicate that De Lank Farm operated an intensive form of agriculture. The reference to Harris working on the farm is, however, incorrect. Probably, the inspector had

FIGURE 37: *Masters' milk van c.1940.* (Courtesy Mrs G. Masters)

recently visited the Harris farm which was in the vicinity. The reference to 'glass houses', in which tomatoes were being grown, is correct. According to the oral testimony of 94-year-old Mrs Grace Masters (wife of the late Charles Masters), there were, in fact, two greenhouses with tomatoes as the main crop, interspersed with early lettuce. In 1940 the farm was no longer allowed to grow its crop of chrysanthemums (for obvious reasons) and their place in the greenhouses was taken by summer beans, carrots and cucumbers. As one would expect, the form also records what land had been ploughed up since 1940.

De Lank Farm in the 1930s and '40s was principally an arable and dairy farm.

As the textual records help to show, it was essentially an arable and dairy farm. Livestock consisted of cows (mostly for milking), sheep, a few pigs and poultry. The farm was of 186 acres with another 100 acres of rough grazing around the quarries. The grazing land actually belonged to the farm, although it is likely that the De Lank Quarries continued to hold the mineral rights. Most of the arable acreage was devoted to corn, although early seed potatoes (actually top grade Scottish seed) were a speciality and turnips were not forgotten! The 'Market Gardens' form, as frequently happened, is crossed through except for the hay and straw section.

The records also reveal that ten workers were employed on the farm. As usual, no names or other details – besides their sex and whether or not they were aged 21 or over – are given. One of the male workers over 21 was, however, known to be Herb Blewitt. Herb lived in one of the tied cottages across the road from the farm and stayed on at the farm throughout his working life. One of the other male workers was a cousin and one of the females, Renee, a Land Girl. The main census form (fig.38) only shows two horses whereas before the war at least four horses were on loan to the quarries. Some of the 'horsepower' lost in this way was made up for by the presence of a 28 hp Fordson tractor – which was, incidentally, still in use on the farm in the 1960s! During the period covered by the Survey, there was an increased emphasis on the use of machinery and the farmers of De Lank were always willing to purchase machinery if they could afford it. It is known that they bought the first milking machine in the area.

MINISTRY OF AGRICULTURE AND FISHERIES.

THE DEFENCE REGULATIONS, 1939, AND THE AGRICULTURAL RETURNS ORDER, 1939.

RETURN WITH RESPECT TO AGRICULTURAL LAND ON 4th JUNE, 1941.

Fill in both Farms R.G.S.S. (Green) and C.47.S.Y. (Blue)

	CROPS AND GRASS	Statute Acres		LIVE STOCK on holding on 4th June, including any sent for sale on that or previous day	Number (in figures)
1	Wheat	9	43	Cows and Heifers in milk	20
2	Barley		44	Cows in Calf, but not in milk	2
3	Oats		45	Heifers in Calf, with first Calf	
4	Mixed Corn with Wheat in mixture		46	Bulls being used for service	1
5	Mixed Corn without Wheat in mixture	2½½	47	Bulls (including Bull Calves) being reared for service	
6	Rye		48	OTHER CATTLE — 2 years old and above { Male	
7	Beans, winter or spring, for stock feeding		49	Female	
8	Peas, for stock feeding, not for human consumption		50	1 year old and under 2 { Male	3
9	Potatoes, first earlies	11	51	Female	8
10	Potatoes, main crop and second earlies	½	52	Under 1 year old:— (a) For rearing (excluding Bull Calves being reared for service)	6
11	Turnips and Swedes, for fodder	3½	53	(b) Intended for slaughter as Calves	
12	Mangolds	1½	54	**TOTAL CATTLE and CALVES**	40
13	Sugar Beet		55	Steers and Heifers over 1 year old being fattened for slaughter before 30th November, 1941	
14	Kale, for fodder		56	SHEEP OVER 1 YEAR OLD — Ewes kept for further breeding (excluding two-tooth Ewes)	64
15	Rape (or Cole)		57	Rams kept for service	2
16	Cabbage, Savoys, and Kohl Rabi, for fodder		58	Two-tooth Ewes (Shearling Ewes or Gimmers) to be put to the ram in 1941	20
17	Vetches or Tares		59	Other Sheep over 1 year old	4
18	Lucerne		60	SHEEP UNDER 1 YEAR OLD — Ewe Lambs to be put to the ram in 1941	
19	Mustard, for seed		61	Ram Lambs for service in 1941	
20	Mustard, for fodder or ploughing in		62	Other Sheep and Lambs under 1 year old	61
21	Flax, for fibre or linseed		63	**TOTAL SHEEP and LAMBS**	151
22	Hops, Statute Acres, not Hop Acres		64	Sows in Pig	
23	Orchards, with crops, fallow, or grass below the trees		65	Gilts in Pig	
24	Orchards, with small fruit below the trees		66	Other Sows kept for breeding	1
25	Small Fruit, not under orchard trees		67	Barren Sows for fattening	
26	Vegetables for human consumption (excluding Potatoes), Flowers and Crops under Glass		68	Boars being used for service	
27	All Other Crops not specified elsewhere on this return or grown on patches of less than ¼ acre		69	ALL OTHER PIGS (not entered above) — Over 5 months old	
28	Bare Fallow		70	2–5 months	
29	Clover, Sainfoin, and Temporary Grasses for Mowing this season	21	71	Under 2 months	7
30	Clover, Sainfoin, and Temporary Grasses for Grazing (not for Mowing this season)	7	72	**TOTAL PIGS**	8
31	Permanent Grass for Mowing this season	5	73	Fowls over 6 months old	180
32	Permanent Grass for Grazing (not for Mowing this season), but excluding rough grazings	73	74	Fowls under 6 months old	45
33	TOTAL OF ABOVE ITEMS, 1 to 32 (Total acreage of Crops and Grass, excluding Rough Grazings)	156	75	POULTRY — Ducks of all ages	
34	Rough Grazings—Mountain, Heath, Moor, or Down Land, or other rough land used for grazing on which the occupier has the sole grazing rights	100	76	If none, write "None" — Geese of all ages	
			77	Turkeys over 6 months old	
			78	Turkeys under 6 months old	

LABOUR actually employed on holding on 4th June. The occupier, his wife, or domestic servants should not be entered.

			Number (in figures)			Number (in figures)
35	WHOLETIME REGULAR WORKERS	Males, 21 years old and over	2	79	**TOTAL POULTRY**	225
36		Males, 18 to 21 years old		80	GOATS OF ALL AGES	
37	If none, write "None"	Males, under 18 years old			HORSES on holding on 4th June	Number (in figures)
38		Women and Girls		81	Horses used for Agricultural Purposes (including Mares kept for breeding) or by Market Gardeners { (a) mares	2
39	CASUAL (SEASONAL or PART-TIME) WORKERS	Males, 21 years old and over	1	82	(b) geldings	2
40		Males, under 21 years old	1	83	Unbroken Horses of 1 year old and above { (a) mares	
41		Women and Girls		84	(b) geldings	
42		**TOTAL WORKERS**	10	85	Light Horses under 1 year old	
			6	86	Heavy Horses under 1 year old	
	Form No. C 47, S.S.Y.			87	Stallions being used for service in 1941	
	M.14060. 4/41. (52-4851)			88	All Other Horses (not entered above)	
				89	**TOTAL HORSES**	2

FIGURE 38: *National Farm Survey Return of Agricultural Land Use for De Lank Farm.* (The National Archives)

■ Locating the maps

The records of the National Farm Survey are held at The National Archives. The easiest way to identify the farm or area one is interested in is to start with the OS-based map (see Series MAF 72 in TNA's catalogue) which numbers the farms. However, if the name of the appropriate parish is known, one can use this, together with the series (MAF 32), to search the on-line catalogue to obtain the parish reference and piece number, which will then lead to the respective textual records.

Since the Primary Record (the field inspector's report) and each type of census return are stored separately, it can be easy to return home having 'forgotten' to look at one of the forms relating to a particular farm. Owing to resistance on the part of some farmers to filling in yet another form, the one asking for information on rent payable, motive power etc., may not be present.

In the case of De Lank, the map was consulted first and then the online search facility was used to locate the paper records. The search returned 31 matches of which one referred to St Breward parish. The search result gave the full reference in order of series/piece number/parish code as MAF32/435/135 (the parish code for St Breward is 135). Browsing through the parish reports, the farm and its parcel reference were then located (in this case the farm code was 34).

More information is given in G. Beech and R. Mitchell, *Maps for Family and Local History: The Records of the Tithe, Valuation Office and National Farm Surveys of England and Wales 1836-1943* (2nd ed., TNA, 2004).

B. Short, C. Watkins, W. Foot and P. Kinsman, *The National Farm Survey 1941-1943: State Surveillance and the Countryside in England and Wales in the Second World War* (CABI Publishing, Wallingford, 1999).

The National Archives has a Research Guide on National Farm Surveys of England and Wales, 1940-1943 (http://www.nationalarchives.gov.uk/catalogue).

Sources for Further Research:

On-line:

The Northumberland Communities website with its host of on-line tithe, Valuation Office Survey and other historical maps
http://communities.northumberland.gov.uk/
Two Villages Archive Trust (Milton Keynes Village)
http://www.mkheritage.co.uk/tva/index.html

Books:

Sarah Bendell, *Dictionary of Land Surveyors and Local Map-makers of Great Britain and Ireland 1530-1850*, 2 vols., 2nd ed. (London, 1997).

D. Bryan, **Ditton Priors. A Settlement of the Brown Clee** (Logaston Press, 2006).

Egham-By-Runneymede Historical Society, **Thorpe. A Surrey Village in Maps** (Surrey Archaeological Society, 2001).

B. Halse, **Levisham: A Case Study in Local History** (Levisham, 2003).

P. Hindle, **Maps for Historians** (Chichester, 1998).

B Short, **Land and Society in Edwardian Britain** (Cambridge, 1997).

Shere Gomshall & Peaslake Local History Society, **Shere. A Surrey Village in Maps.** (Surrey Archaeological Society, 2001).

Smith, D., **Maps and Plans for the Local Historian and Collector: a Guide to the Types of Maps of the British Isles produced before 1914** (1988).

Hilary M Thomas, **A Catalogue of Glamorgan Estate Maps** (Cardiff, 1992).

H.Wallis, H. and A. McConnell,(eds.). **Historians' Guide to Early British Maps: A Guide to the Location of Pre-1900 maps of the British Isles preserved in the United Kingdom and Ireland** (Royal Historical Society, 1994).

Front Cover: John Rocque's county map of Berkshire (1761). (Berkshire Record Office).

Index

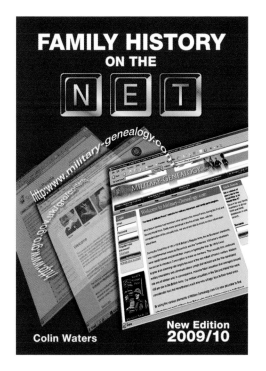

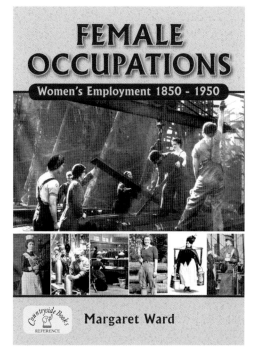

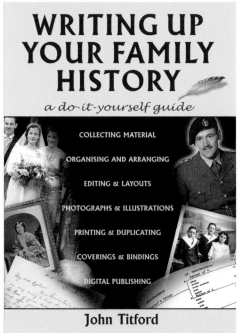

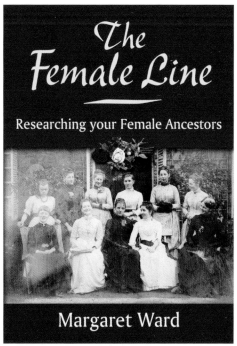

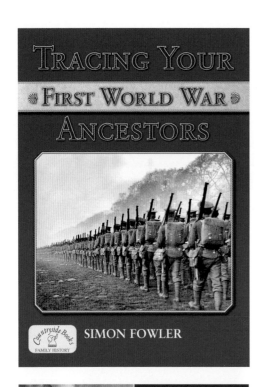

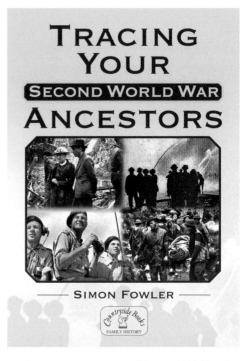

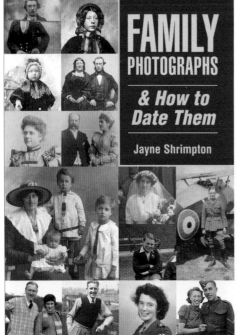

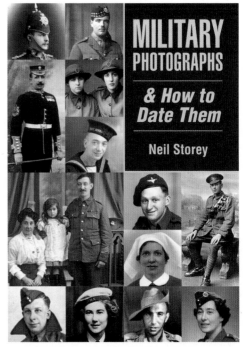

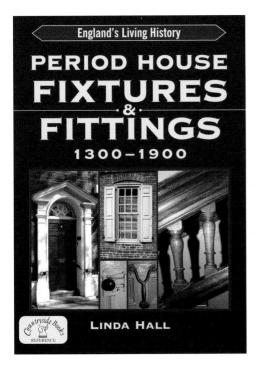

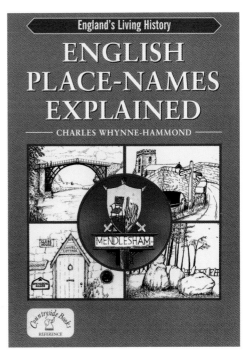

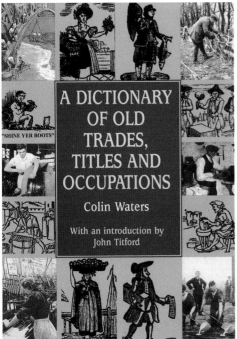

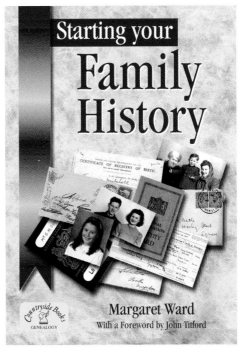